NATEF Correlated Task Sheets
to accompany

Automatic Transmissions and Transaxles

Fourth Edition

Tom Birch
Chuck Rockwood

Prentice Hall

Upper Saddle River, New Jersey
Columbus, Ohio

Editor-in-Chief: Vernon Anthony
Acquisitions Editor: Wyatt Morris
Editorial Assistant: Christopher Reed
Project Manager: Holly Shufeldt
Art Director: Candace Rowley
Cover photo: Courtesy of iStockphoto
Operations Specialist: Laura Weaver
Director of Marketing: David Gesell
Marketing Assistant: Les Roberts

This book was printed and bound by Quebecor Printing. The cover was printed by Demand Production Center.

Pearson Education Ltd., London
Pearson Education Singapore Pte. Ltd.
Pearson Education Canada, Inc.
Pearson Education—Japan

Pearson Education Australia Pty. Limited
Pearson Education North Asia Ltd. , Hong Kong
Pearson Educación de Mexico, S.A. de C.V.
Pearson Education Malaysia Pte. Ltd.

10 9 8 7 6 5 4 3 2 1

Prentice Hall
is an imprint of

www.pearsonhighered.com

ISBN-13: 978-0-13-506953-0
ISBN-10:   0-13-506953-X

Preface

This worktext contains lab exercises to guide you through practical, live service operations. The exercises contain tips, cautions, procedures, rules-of-thumb, and anticipated results. They are designed to be used with the textbook *AUTOMATIC TRANSMISSIONS AND TRANSAXLES, FOURTH EDITION.* The exercises are arranged in the same order as the text's service chapters.

The tasks described in the exercises are those commonly used in this service industry. Most of them are also considered to be priority one (P1) tasks by the National Automotive Technicians Education Foundation (NATEF), the educational branch of ASE. Appendix 2 is a correlation of the NATEF tasks to the exercises. Most of the priority one (P1), two (P2), and three (P3) tasks are also covered by these exercises.

The appendix includes precautions that should be observed when working on automotive drive trains.

Thomas (Tom) Birch, Charles (Chuck) Rockwood

TABLE OF CONTENTS

E 1, MATERIAL SAFETY DATA SHEET(MSDS) WORKSHEET

Name_____ **Date**_____

Make/Model_____ **Year**_____ **Instructor's OK**_____

_____ 1. Where are the MSDS sheets located at your facility?

_____

_____ 2. Identify three chemicals or solvents that are commonly used in an automotive repair shop.

A. _____

B. _____

C. _____

Record the following information about them from the MSDS:

A. Product name _____

    Chemical name(s) _____

    Does the material contain "chlor" (chlorine) or "fluor" (fluorine) which
    may indicate it is a hazardous material? **Yes** _____ **No** _____

    Flash point = _____ degrees (Best, if above 140° F/60° C)

    pH = _____ (7 = neutral, greater than 7 = caustic, lower than 7 = acid)

B. Product name _____

    Chemical name(s) _____

    Does the material contain "chlor" (chlorine) or "fluor" (fluorine) which
    may indicate it is a hazardous material? **Yes** _____ **No** _____

    Flash point = _____ degrees (Best, if above 140° F/60° C)

    pH = _____ (7 = neutral, greater than 7 = caustic, lower than 7 = acid)

C. Product name _____

    Chemical name(s) _____

    Does the material contain "chlor" (chlorine) or "fluor" (fluorine) which
    may indicate it is a hazardous material? **Yes** _____ **No** _____

    Flash point = _____ degrees (Best, if above 140° F/60° C)

    pH = _____ (7 = neutral, greater than 7 = caustic, lower than 7 = acid)

_____ 3. If a hazardous spill should occur, who is the first person to contact at your:

    School: _____

    Workplace: _____

E 2, PRESSURE, TEMPERATURE, AND WEIGHT CONVERSION

Name_____ **Date**_____

Make/Model_____ **Year**_____ **Instructor's OK** _____

Directions: Convert the following measurements

Note: Conversation tables can be found in Appendix 3.

_____1. 60 psi to kilopascal (kPa): _____ kPa

_____ 2. 60 psi to bar: _____ bar

_____ 3. 500 kPa to psi: _____ psi

_____ 4. 100° Fahrenheit (F) to Celsius (C): _____ °C

_____ 5. 80° C to °F: _____ °F

_____ 6. 20 pounds (lb) to ounces (oz): _____ oz

_____ 7. 20 lb to kilograms (kg): _____ kg

_____ 8. 20 kg to oz: _____ oz

_____ 9. 20 kg to lb: _____ lb

_____ 10. 4 quarts (qt) to liters (l): _____ liters

_____ 11. 6 l to quarts: _____ quarts

_____ 12. 6 l to pints: _____ pints

E 3, COMPLETE WORK ORDER

Meets NATEF Task: (A-1) Complete work order to include customer information, vehicle identifying information, customer concern, related service history, cause, and correction. (P-1)

Name_____ **Date**_____

Make/Model_____ **Year**_____ **Instructor's OK** _____

Note: A work order, also called a repair order or RO, is used by a repair shop to provide:
- the customer concern and related vehicle history to the technician
- a written repair (parts and labor) cost estimate to the customer, and
- the final parts and labor cost of the repair to the customer.

A sample repair order is on the back; complete the repair order for the following customer:

Mr. Billy Battles' 1998 Ford F150 2WD pickup (134,987 miles) has been working well up until recently. Now, it seems to have a delayed and very soft neutral to drive shift. He is not sure what is causing the problem, and he would like the shop diagnose and repair the problem. You start by opening a repair order and asking a few questions to define the problem and to get necessary vehicle information. From the information, you feel that the hydraulic pressure in this 4R70W transmission is low and the repair will be to check the fluid level and condition and the pressures.. You also feel that it would be a good idea to change the fluid and replace the filter and pan gasket. The truck has a V-8 4.6L VIN 6 engine.

Mr. Battles lives at 5467 South Ridge Road, Littleburg, PA 12345, and his phone number is (798) 654-3210. The truck's license number is W98765.

You explain to Mr. Battles that there will be a one hour charge for diagnosis, which includes pressure testing. You also mention that the shop labor rate is $75.00 per hour, and all parts will have an 8% tax. The repair will be to inspect the valve body. The Labor Guide recommends 0.9 hours to remove and replace the transmission pan and filter and 0.9 hours to remove and replace the valve body. You recommend an additional 0.3 hours to adjust the manual and throttle linkage. The parts, from a local parts store, are pan gasket: $ 6.85, valve body gaskets: $2.96, and four quarts of fluid at $6.95 per quart.

_____ 1. Fill out the customer and vehicle information and your cost estimate sections of the work order using the information given above.

You called Mr. Battles at 9:30 AM to get authorization for the repair, and he told you to go ahead with the repair but to skip adjusting the manual and throttle linkage. Your pressure test showed low fluid pressure, and you found the valve body bolts were loose. You removed the valve body, cleaned the exterior, replaced the gaskets, replaced the valve body, tightening the bolts to the proper torque, completing the job. You completed the repair order and called Mr. Battles to pick up his truck.

_____ 2. Complete the repair order.

Customer Information

Daytime _____

Evening _____

Name _____

Address _____

City _____ State _____ Zip _____

Vehicle Information Make _____

Year _____ Model _____

Color _____ Mileage _____

VIN _____

Materials

Customer Concern

Related Service History

Labor Performed

Root Cause of Problem

Totals

Materials _____

Labor _____

Misc. _____

Sub Total _____

Tax _____

TOTAL _____

Customer Authorization

X _____

Original Estimate: _____

Revised Estimate: _____

E 4, IDENTIFY VEHICLE AND DRIVE TRAIN COMPONENTS

Meets NATEF Task: (A-4) Locate and interpret vehicle and major component identification numbers (VIN, vehicle certification labels, calibration decals). (P-1)

Name_____ Date_____

Make/Model_____ Year_____ Instructor's OK_____

_____1. Locate the vehicle VIN (Vehicle Identification Number). It is located on top of the instrument panel on the left/driver's side.

VIN: _____

_____2. Using the VIN, identify the country of origin and year model for this vehicle?
Tip: The first character (letter or number) indicates the country of origin.
Tip: The tenth character indicates the year.

Country of origin: _____

Model year: _____

_____3. Locate the Vehicle Certification label. It is often located on the edge of the driver's door or door jam. What is the Gross Vehicle Weight-Rating (GVWR)

GVWR: _____

_____4. Locate the engine, transmission, and if applicable, drive axle codes.
Note: In some vehicles, these are on a body code plate along with other codes, like paint. On other vehicles, they are on decals/tags that are attached to the engine, transmission, or drive axle.

Engine Code: _____, Engine Type and Size: _____

Transmission Code: _____, Transmission ID: _____

Drive Axle Code: _____, Drive Axle ID: _____

_____5. Determine the type of drive train (check all that apply).

_____ FWD _____ Manual Transmission _____ Manual Transfer Case

_____ RWD	_____ Automatic Trans.	_____ Automatic/Electric Transfer Case
_____ 4WD	_____ CVT	_____ Limited Slip Drive Axle
_____ AWD	_____ EVT	

_____ 3-Speed _____ 4-Speed _____ 5-Speed _____ 6-Speed _____ 7-Speed

_____6. Determine the fluid type that should be used in the transmission.

Fluid Type: _____

_____7. Determine the fluid type that should be used in the drive axle(s) or final drive section of the transaxle.

Fluid Type: _____

_____8. Locate service information for this vehicle and system and determine if there are any TSBs (Technical Service Bulletins) that apply to this vehicle's drivetrain.

Information Source: _____ **Section:** _____

TSB(s): _____

E 5, RESEARCH SERVICE INFORMATION

Meets NATEF Task: (A-3) Research applicable vehicle service information, such as transmission/transaxle system operation, fluid type, vehicle service history, service precautions, and technical service bulletins. (P-1)

Name_____ Date_____

Make/Model_____ Year_____ Instructor's OK_____

_____ 1. Locate automatic transmission service information.

Information source: _____
Section: _____

Mainline fluid pressure
Drive: _____, **Reverse:** _____

Input shaft endplay: _____

Fluid capacity: _____ quarts, liters **Fluid type:** _____

Researching information from a service manual

_____ 2. Locate automatic transmission related technical service bulletins (TSBs).

A. Topic: _____
Bulletin Number: _____

Problem/Correction:

_____

_____

_____

Service Engine Soon Light with Stored Codes P0112, P0113, P111 or P1112 (Replace IAT Sensor Connector) #02-06-03-005 - (06/05/2002)

A TSB

B. Topic _____
Bulletin Number: _____

Problem/Correction: _____

_____ 3. Research the vehicle's service history and record all previous automatic transmission system-related service or repairs.

_____

_____

_____

_____

_____ 4. If you have access to the Internet, visit each of these sites and locate the indicated information:

www.acdelco.com
Who owns/manages this site: _____
What is their major product: _____
How many links to other transmission sites are provided: _____

www.atra.com
Who owns/manages this site: _____
What is their major product: _____
How many links to other transmission sites are provided: _____

http://members.iatn.net
Who owns/manages this site: _____
What is their major product: _____
How many links to other transmission sites are provided: _____

www.pennzoil.com
Who owns/manages this site: _____
What is their major product: _____
How many links to other transmission sites are provided: _____

www.sonnax.com
Who owns/manages this site: _____
What is their major product: _____
How many links to other transmission sites are provided: _____

www.raybestosproducts.com
Who owns/manages this site: _____
What is their major product: _____
How many links to other transmission sites are provided: _____

E 6, CHECK FLUID LEVEL
AND CONDITION

Meets NATEF Task: (A-5) Diagnose fluid loss and condition concerns; check fluid level on transmissions with and without dipstick; determine necessary action. (P-1)

Name_____ Date_____

Make/Model_____Year_____ Instructor's OK _____

_____1. Locate the procedure for checking transmission fluid in this vehicle.

      Information source: _____ **Section:**_____ **Page:**_____

_____2. Identify the fluid type recommended:

      _____

_____3. What is the fluid capacity?

      Change:_____

      Refill:_____

_____4. Check the fluid level.

      Tip: Transmissions that do not have dipsticks have a fluid level plug for the correct fluid level. Fluid should barely run out of the opening when it is at operating temperature. Operating temperature can be easily checked using an infrared thermometer.

      Transmission gear range? _____

      Engine running?   **Yes _____ No _____**

      Was the vehicle on level ground?   **Yes _____ No _____**

      Dip Stick:

      OK _____ Low _____ High _____

      What was the fluid temperature? **Hot _____ Cold _____**

      Level Plug:

OK _____ **Low** _____ **High** _____

Plug location: **Pan** _____ **Case** _____

What was the fluid temperature? _____ **Degrees F, C (circle one)**

_____5. Inspect the fluid condition.
   Tip: If the fluid appears dirty, place a few drops on a white, absorbent (blotter) paper.
   The fluid will be absorbed and any deposits will be visible on the paper.

Smell: **OK** _____ **Old/varnish** _____ **burned** _____ **Other** _____

Color: **Normal** _____ **Darkened** _____ **Pink** _____ **Other** _____

Deposits/debris: **OK** _____ **Contaminated** _____ **Foam** _____ **Other**_____

Did you do a blotter check? Yes _____ **No** _____ **Results?** _____

If no, why not? _____

_____6. What was the appearance of the dipstick after you wiped it clean?

OK/clean metal _____ **varnished** _____

_____7. What is your recommendation for the transmission based on the fluid inspection?

_____

_____

E 7, CHANGE FLUID AND FILTER

Meets NATEF Task: (A-5) Diagnose fluid loss and condition concerns; check fluid level in transmissions with and without dip-stick; determine necessary action. (P-1)

Name_____ Date_____

Make/Model_____ Year_____ Instructor's OK_____

_____1. Locate the automatic transmission fluid change procedure for this vehicle.

Information source: _____ **Section:**_____ **Page:**_____

Fluid type: _____ **Fluid capacity:** _____ **Internal filter: Yes ___ No ___**

_____2. Raise the vehicle if necessary to gain access to the transmission.
Note: It is recommended to operate the vehicle until the fluid is at operating temperature. The hot fluid will carry more foreign particles as it is drained.

_____3. Remove the parts of the vehicle necessary to gain access to the transmission pan. Position a drain container under the pan.
Tip: Some vehicles have a drain plug so it is not necessary to remove the transmission pan to change the fluid, although most automatic transmissions have the filter inside the pan that should be changed.
Tip: Some shops use a fluid evacuator to pull the fluid out of the filler tube. This is used to prevent a fluid spill.

_____4. Determine the best direction to lower the pan, and loosen two of the pan bolts that will serve as a hinge. Remove the remaining bolts in such a way that the desired side of the pan lowers slowly, in a controlled manner.

_____5. When most of the fluid has spilled out of the pan, hold the pan level and remove the remaining two bolts and the pan.
Tip: Note how much fluid was drained from the transmission; you will be replacing the same amount back into it.

Fluid Level
Leave two bolts in this side.
Loosen and remove all the others.

Fluid Spill
Slowly loosen the two remaining bolts

When fluid spill stops, remove the remaining bolts and the pan

Tip: A few vehicles have a drain plug in the torque converter; removing this plug allows you remove more of the old fluid.

_____6. Clean the pan, and inspect the pan and the magnet that might be inside.

OK _____ **NOT OK** _____

If NOT OK, what debris did you find? _____

_____7. Remove the filter and gasket/seal (if used).
 Tip: Be prepared for fluid to spill as the filter is removed.
 Tip: Some filters can be easily opened, and the filter material can be checked to see what debris has been trapped.

_____8. Install the new gasket/seal and filter. Tighten any retaining bolts to the correct torque.
 Tip: Rubber seals can be easily installed if they are covered with a thin film of ATF or transmission assembly lube.

_____9. Check the pan to insure that the gasket surface is flat, and straighten it if necessary.

OK _____ **NOT OK** _____

_____10. Place the new gasket in position on the pan, and start several of the pan bolts through the gasket to hold it in position. Raise the pan into position, and turn each of the bolts into the transmission several rotations.
 Tip: Do not tighten any of the pan bolts until they all are installed.

_____11. Tighten the pan bolts to the proper torque.

Specified torque: _____

_____12. Pour enough fluid into the transmission so that it shows on the dipstick.

_____13. Start the engine, and with your foot firmly on the brake pedal, shift the transmission through the gears. Once again, check the transmission fluid level and add fluid as needed to bring it to the correct level.
 Tip: Transmissions that do not have dipsticks may have a fluid level plug for the correct fluid level. Fluid should barely run out of the opening when it is at operating temperature. Operating temperature can be easily checked using an infrared thermometer.

E 8, EXCHANGE TRANSMISSION FLUID

Meets NATEF Task: (B-6) Service transmission, perform visual inspection, replace fluids and filters . (P-1)

Name_____ Date_____

Make/Model_____ Year_____ Instructor's OK _____

Note: Many shops are avoiding in-vehicle transmission pan removal because of the possibility of a fluid spill. Fluid exchange units are available that can be connected to the vehicle with two simple connections. These units can quickly flush the used fluid from the transmission as new fluid replaces it.

_____1. Locate the transmission fluid capacity and type for this vehicle.

Fluid Capacity: _____ **Fluid Type:**_____

_____2. Following the directions of the fluid exchange unit, determine how much fluid will be needed for the transmission. Check to insure that there is adequate fluid in the exchanger .

Fluid required: _____
Fluid available: _____

_____3. Determine how the fluid exchange unit connects to the vehicle and what adapters will be used.

Connection At:
Radiator/cooler: _____
Transmission: _____
Other: _____

_____4. Determine how the waste fluid will be captured.
Tip: Make sure that there is enough room in the waste fluid container for the fluid from the transmission.

In the exchange unit: _____, **In a separate container:** _____

_____5. Connect the lines/hoses from the fluid exchange unit to the vehicle.

_____6. Operate the exchange unit to remove the old fluid and replace it with new fluid.

_____7. Disconnect the fluid exchange unit from the vehicle.

_____8. Start the vehicle's engine to check fluid level.

    OK _____ NOT OK _____

_____9. Start the vehicle's engine to check for leaks.

    OK _____ NOT OK _____

_____10. Recycle or dispose of the waste fluid in the approved manner.

E 9, INSPECT FOR FLUID LEAKS AND LOCATE SOURCE

Meets NATEF Task: (A-5) Diagnose fluid loss and condition concerns; check fluid level on transmissions with and without dip-stick; determine necessary action. (P-1)

Name_____ Date_____

Make/Model_____ Year_____ Instructor's OK _____

_____1. Identify the color of these fluids.

    Fluid type: ATF: _____ Engine Oil:_____ Coolant:_____

_____2. Park the vehicle over a section of very clean, smooth floor or place a large sheet of paper under the vehicle. Run the engine for about 15 minutes or until you notice fluid dripping.
Tip: The arrows indicate the possible leak locations.

    Fluid drips: Yes _____
                 No _____

_____3. Raise the vehicle so you can inspect the area above the fluid drips or where you suspect the leak to be.
Tip: A mirror can be used to look into hidden areas.

    Leak located: Yes _____
                  No _____

    Record the leak source at Step 10.

_____4. If the leak cannot be located, clean the transmission and cooler lines. Operate the vehicle for several miles in all transmission ranges. Operate the vehicle in park at various speeds. Repeat Step 3.
Tip: If the leak location still cannot be located exactly, fluorescent dye can be added to the fluid or the suspected leak area can be coated with powder to help find the leak.

    Leak located: Yes _____ No _____

    Record the leak source at Step 10.

Black Light:

_____5. Add the specified amount of tracer dye into the transmission, and operate the vehicle as directed by the dye kit.

_____6. Raise the vehicle, and shine the ultraviolet (UV) black light on the area where you suspect the transmission is leaking.
Tip: The dye will glow under the UV light, making the leak easier to find.
Tip: If you suspect the leak is in a hidden area, wipe the area using a shop cloth, and shine the UV light on the cloth. A leak is indicated if the cloth glows.

Leak located: Yes _____ No _____

Record the leak source at Step 10.

Powder:

_____7. Spray an aerosol foot powder on the area of the transmission where you think the leak is located.
Tip: You need a thin, even coating of powder on the surface of the suspected leak area.

_____8. Operate the vehicle for several miles in all transmission ranges and in park at various speeds.

_____9. Raise the vehicle and inspect the area where the foot powder was applied.
Tip: An ATF leak will show up as a reddish stain on the powder coating.

Leak located: Yes _____ No _____

Record the leak source at Step 10.

_____10. Indicate the leak location.

Pan gasket _____	Oil cooler connection _____	Front pump seal _____
Case gasket _____	Driveshaft seal _____	Speed sensor seal _____
Filler pipe seal _____	Pressure tap plug _____	Wiring connector seal _____
TV cable seal _____	Manual shaft seal _____	Governor cover seal _____
Accumulator Cover _____		
Other _____		

E 10, ADJUST SHIFT LINKAGE

Meets NATEF Task: (B-1) Inspect, adjust, or replace manual valve shift linkage; transmission range sensor/switch, and park/neutral position switch. (P-2)

Name_____ **Date**_____

Make/Model_____ **Year**_____ **Instructor's OK** _____

_____1. Locate the shift linkage adjustment procedure for this vehicle.

Transmission model: _____

Information source: _____ **Section:**_____ **Page:**_____

_____2. Check for proper cable/linkage movement.
Tip: The shift lever should move smoothly through its travel without excess effort. You should be able to feel the detents operate inside the transmission.
Tip: Too much effort usually indicates cable bind; the shift cable and housing probably should be replaced.

OK _____ **NOT OK** _____

_____3. Check for proper starter operation.
Tip: The starter should operate only in park and neutral.

OK _____ **NOT OK** _____

_____4. Check for proper shift lock operation.
Tip: In most vehicles, you should not be able to remove the ignition key unless the transmission is shifted into park. After inserting the ignition key, you should not be able to shift out of park unless the brakes are applied.

OK _____ **NOT OK** _____

_____5. Turn the ignition to key on, engine off position. Then move the manual lever through each of the gear positions as you watch the gear position indicator and feel the detent notches. The shift indicator positions should line up with the detent notches.

OK _____ **NOT OK** _____

Shift Cable
Adjuster
Manual Lever

_____6. Shift the manual lever into the recommended gear position. Locate the adjuster on the cable or linkage.
Tip: On most RWD vehicles, the vehicle must be raised to gain access to the adjustment.

_____7. Loosen the adjuster, and move the manual lever to the proper position. Tighten the adjuster to the proper torque.
Tip: After adjusting, make sure the shift into park occurs easily and completely.

_____8. Repeat Step 5 to insure proper adjustment.

E 11, ADJUST THROTTLE LINKAGE

Name_____ Date_____

Make/Model_____ Year_____ Instructor's OK _____

_____1. Locate the throttle valve (TV) adjustment procedure for this vehicle.

Information source: _____ **Section:**_____ **Page:**_____

_____2. Determine if this vehicle uses a mechanical rod or cable linkage and the adjuster location.
Tip: When replacing a TV cable, make sure that your replacement cable is the correct length.

      Rod : Yes____ No ____
      Cable: Yes____ No ____
      Other: _____

_____3. Operate the throttle to make sure that it moves smoothly from idle to wide open throttle (WOT) and returns smoothly to idle. Operate the TV linkage to make sure that it also moves smoothly and completely.
Tip: TV linkage that does not operate smoothly can cause erratic shift quality and/or shift timing.

OK _____ NOT OK _____

_____4. Follow the manufacturer's directions to adjust the TV linkage as needed. After adjusting, operate the TV linkage to insure that it still has complete travel.
Tip: Some vehicle manufacturer's recommend the TV linkage be adjusted to obtain a specified TV fluid pressure.

_____5. Road test the vehicle to make sure that the shift points are correct.
Tip: With most transmissions, a TV cable that is too long can cause early and/or soft shifts. A TV cable that is too short can cause late and/or harsh shifts. This will be reversed on some vehicles.

Test drive results:
      Shift timing: OK _____ **Early** _____ **Late** _____

      Shift quality: OK _____ **Soft** _____ **Harsh** _____

E 12, ADJUST BAND

Name_____ **Date**_____

Make/Model_____ **Year**_____ **Instructor's OK** _____

Note: Some automatic transmissions use a threaded band adjuster. Others use a selective servo apply pin. The correct length pin is selected to get the proper band clearance. Selective pins require a gauging procedure. This exercise describes band adjustment using threaded adjusters; selective pin adjustment is usually done as part of a transmission repair.

_____1. Locate the band adjustment procedure for this vehicle.

Information source: _____ **Section:**_____ **Page:**_____

_____2. Are special tools or
gauges required for this
adjustment?

Yes _____
No _____

_____3. Raise the vehicle to gain
access to the adjustment.

_____4. If necessary, drain the
fluid and remove the pan.

Locknut

Rear Band Adjusting Screw

_____5. Loosen the adjuster screw lock nut, and turn the adjuster screw inward the required
amount.
*Note: This step should apply the
band completely.*
*Tip: Mark the adjuster screw so you
can easily count the number of turns
that the adjuster is rotated. This will
give you an indication of band wear
and lets you return to the starting
point if necessary.*

**Adjustment screw tightening
specification:** _____

Number of turns inward:

_____

**Wrench holding
locknut**

**Torque wrench and socket
turning adjuster screw**

_____6. Back off the adjustment screw the required number of turns.
Note: This should provide the correct band clearance.

Number of turns outward: _____

_____7. Tighten the locknut to the specified torque.

Locknut torque specification: _____

Note: The vehicle should be driven to insure that the band applied and releases correctly. A loose band will cause a delayed or loose shift. A tight band will cause a drag in the gear ranges where it should be released.

_____8. Test drive results.

Loose/Slipping Shift: _____ **Tight/Drag:** _____ **OK:** _____

E 13, VOLT-OHMMETER USAGE

Meets NATEF Task: (A-12) Diagnose electronic transmission/transaxle systems using appropriate test equipment and service information. (P-2)

Name_____ Date_____

Make/Model_____ Year_____ Instructor's OK _____

Note: Electrical meters are normally used to check electrical circuits and components. Proper usage is necessary for accurate results.

Voltmeter:

_____ 1. Select DC volts, and connect the voltmeter leads to a vehicle's battery observing the correct polarity. Read the meter to determine the voltage.
Tip: If the vehicle has been operated Recently, expect 12.6 V.

Volts: _____
OK _____ NOT OK _____

_____ 2. Turn on the headlights. Measure the voltage, and record the meter readings at the following time intervals:
Tip: Stop this test if the voltage goes below 10.5 v.

15 seconds _____, 30 sec. _____, 45 sec. _____, 1 min. _____

_____ 3. Turn off the headlights, start the engine. Measure and record the meter readings at the at the following time intervals:

Immediately: _____, 30 sec. _____, 1 min. _____

_____ 4. Locate the backup light fuse. Measure and record the voltage on both sides of the fuse.
Tip: Some modern vehicles will not allow backup lights unless the engine is running.
Caution: Make sure that the meter wires and other things are out of the way of the pulleys, drive belt, or hot exhaust manifold.

Connector Check Point

Fuse Check Points

Key Off: _____, _____

Key On: _____ , _____

Engine Running: _____ , _____

Ohmmeter:

Note: An ohmmeter must never be connected to a circuit that has power: external voltage will damage the meter. Disconnect the component from the circuit before testing.

_____ 5. Locate a known good relay. Select the Ohms (Ω) scale, on the meter. Connect the leads to the control circuit connectors and read the resistance indicated on the meter. *Tip: With most single relays, two of the connections are for the controlling circuit and two or three are for the switched circuit.*

Control Circuit Connections are: _____ **and** _____
Switched Circuit Connections are: _____ **and** _____
Control circuit resistance: _____ **Ohms**

_____ 6. Reverse the two meter leads, and read the resistance indicated on the meter. *Tip: A different amount of resistance between Steps 5 and 6 indicates that a diode is in this circuit.*

Reversed Resistance: _____ **Ohms**

Is there a diode? Yes _____ **No** _____

_____ 6. Measure the resistance of the switched circuit.

Switched circuit resistance: _____

Tip: If the measured resistance of the switched circuit is "0," the relay is a normally closed relay (NC). If the measured resistance is infinite or "OL," the relay is normally open (NO).

_____ 7. Is the relay normally open or normally closed?

NO _____ **NC** _____

E 14, CHECK TRANSMISSION CONTROL MODULE POWER AND GROUND

Meets NATEF Task: (A-12) Diagnose electronic transmission/transaxle systems using appropriate test equipment and service information. (P-2)

Name_____ Date_____

Make/Model_____ Year_____ Instructor's OK _____

_____1. Locate the transmission wiring diagram and component locator for this vehicle.

Wiring diagram
Information source: _____, Section:_____, Page:_____

Component locater
Information source: _____, Section:_____, Page:_____

_____2. Locate the transmission fuse(s).

Fuse locations and current ratings:

_____

_____

_____3. Locate any transmission relays.

Are there any relays? Yes _____ No _____

_____

If yes, Relay location: _____

_____4. Locate the transmission control module (TCM) and the TCM battery positive (B+) terminals .

TCM location: _____

TCM B+ terminal number: _____

_____5. Connect the negative lead of a voltmeter to a good ground and measure the voltage at each side of each fuse.
Note: With some vehicles, the engine must be running to power the TCM.
Tip: Each measurement should be almost the same as battery voltage. You can allow a slight voltage drop for each connection leading to the fuse.

Fuse condition: OK _____ NOT OK _____, Explain: _____

_____6. Locate the TCM relay, and measure the voltage at the switch B+ terminal.

OK _____ NOT OK _____

Tip: *The measurement should be same as battery voltage. Although, a slight voltage drop for each connection leading to the relay is acceptable.*
Tip: *Leave the connector connected, and if possible, contact (back probe) the metal connector with the voltmeter probe. The alternative is to pierce the wire and seal the hole after making your measurement.*
Tip: *The hole through the insulation can be sealed with clear fingernail polish.*

_____7. Measure the voltage at the TCM B+ terminals.

OK _____ NOT OK _____

_____8. Locate the TCM ground terminal(s), and measure the voltage at each one.
Tip: *Each measurement should be 0V. A slight voltage (0.1V) for the ground connection is acceptable.*

OK _____ NOT OK _____

_____9. Check the transmission ground. Measure the voltage drop between the transmission case and battery ground.
Tip: *Each measurement should be 0V. A slight voltage drop is acceptable (0.2 V or less).*

OK _____ NOT OK _____

NATEF

E 15, IDENTIFY TRANSMISSION ELECTRONIC CONTROLS

Meets NATEF Task: (A-12) Diagnose electronic transmission/transaxle systems using appropriate test equipment and service information. (P-2)

Name_____ Date_____

Make/Model_____ Year_____ Instructor's OK _____

_____1. Locate the automatic transmission wiring diagram and component locator.

Wiring diagram
Information source: _____ **Section:**_____ **Page:**_____

Component locator
Information source: _____ **Section:**_____ **Page:**_____

_____2. Indicate the solenoids used in this transmission.

Torque Converter Clutch: Yes _____ **No** _____

Pressure Control: Yes _____ **No** _____

Shift (How Many?): _____

Other: _____

_____3. Determine if the control system uses Ground Side (B-) or Hot Side (B+) switching.

Ground Side Switched: _____ **Hot Side Switched:** _____

_____4. Determine the style of TCM used.

Separate TCM: _____

TCM is integrated with ECM, engine control module: _____

TCM is integrated with PCM, powertrain control module: _____

Other, Identify: _____

_____5. Where is the TCM located?

Under hood: _____ **Under the instrument panel:** _____

Behind the left kick panel: _____ **Behind the right kick panel:** _____

Under the center consul: _____ **Under seat:** _____

Other, Identify: _____

_____6. How many electrical connectors are used on the transmission?
How many pins/terminals are used at each connector?

Connectors: _____

Pins: _____, _____, _____

_____7. In the list below, identify the sensors used with this transmission. Indicate whether a sensor or switch is used by striking out the appropriate word.

Vehicle Speed Sensor/Switch:	Yes _____	No _____
Manual Lever Position Sensor/Switch:	Yes _____	No _____
Input Speed Sensor/Switch:	Yes _____	No _____
Park Reverse Neutral Drive Low Sensor/Switch:	Yes _____	No _____
Output Speed Sensor/Switch:	Yes _____	No _____
Power Economy Sensor/Switch:	Yes _____	No _____
Fluid Temperature Sensor/Switch:	Yes _____	No _____
Fluid Pressure Sensor/Switch:	Yes _____	No _____
Overdrive Lockout Sensor/Switch:	Yes _____	No _____
Brake On/Off Sensor/Switch:	Yes _____	No _____
Throttle Position Sensor/Switch:	Yes _____	No _____
Engine Coolant Temperature Sensor/Switch:	Yes _____	No _____
Engine Manifold Pressure Sensor/Switch:	Yes _____	No _____

Other, Identify: _____

E 16, COMPLETE TRANSMISSION DIAGNOSIS

Name_____ **Date**_____

Make/Model_____ **Year**_____ **Instructor's OK** _____

Note: This exercise requires information from Exercises 17, 18, 19, & 20. Transmission operation can be affected by the fluid level as well as manual shift linkage, throttle valve, and band adjustments. A quick check of these should be performed as part of every diagnosis.

_____1. Locate the transmission diagnostic check procedure for this vehicle.

    Information source: _____ **Section:**_____ **Page:**_____

_____2. Check the fluid level and condition.

    Fluid level: OK _____ **High** _____ **Low** _____

    Condition: OK _____ **NOT OK** _____ **Explain** _____

_____3. Perform a visual under-hood transmission inspection (recent engine work, engine running condition, vacuum hose condition, and routing).

    OK _____ **NOT OK** _____, **Explain** _____

_____4. If the vehicle is equipped with mechanical throttle linkage, operate the throttle linkage, throttle valve linkage, and kick down linkage to make sure that they operate smoothly and completely.
    Tip: As you operate the throttle valve linkage, you should be able to feel the throttle valve spring inside the transmission. The linkage should bottom out at wide-open-throttle (WOT). Adjust the throttle linkage as described in E 11 if needed.

    OK _____ **NOT OK** _____, **Explain** _____

_____5. Quick check the manual shift linkage.
    Tip: As you shift through the gear ranges, you should feel the internal detents and they should line up with the shift indicator. Adjust the shift linkage as described in E 10 if needed.

    OK _____ **NOT OK** _____, **Explain** _____

_____6. Complete *Exercise 17, Perform Road Test.*

OK _____ **NOT OK** _____ **, Explain** _____

_____7. Complete *Exercise 18, Diagnose NVH Concern.*

OK _____ **NOT OK** _____ **, Explain** _____

_____8. Complete *Exercise 19, Check Hydraulic System Pressures.*

OK _____ **NOT OK** _____ **, Explain** _____

_____9. Complete *Exercise 20, Perform a Stall Test.*

OK _____ **NOT OK** _____ **, Explain** _____

_____10. If the transmission uses a vacuum modulator, Complete *Exercise 21, Check Vacuum Modulator Operation.*

OK _____ **NOT OK** _____ **, Explain** _____

_____11. Determine the condition of this transmission.
   Tip: An air test (E 22) can be performed to locate or confirm internal transmission failure.

OK _____ **NOT OK** _____ **, Explain** _____

_____12. After completing the diagnosis, what do think has caused the concern with this transmission?

_____

_____

_____

_____13. What should be done to repair this transmission?

_____

_____

_____

E 17, PERFORM ROAD TEST

Name_____ **Date**_____

Make/Model_____ **Year**_____ **Instructor's OK** _____

Note: Follow each of these recommendations as you perform this test:
- Check the tires, brakes, and steering to make sure that the vehicle is safe to operate.
- Observe all traffic laws and regulations.
- If serious transmission problems become evident, stop the test to prevent further damage.
- Make sure the vehicle is at normal operating temperatures before beginning.
- Check the engine for abnormal operation.

_____1. Locate the shift point specifications for this vehicle.

    Information source: _____ **Section:**_____ **Page:**_____

_____2. Check the fluid level and condition.

    Level: OK _____ **High** _____ **Low** _____

    Condition: OK _____ **Concern** _____
    Needs Attention _____ **Explain:** _____

    _____

The electrical portion controls the shift points and hydraulic pressure.

The hydraulic portion performs the shifts, applies the TCC, and keeps the geartrain lubricated.

Electrical/ Electronic   Hydraulic

Mechanical

The mechanical portion provides the gear ratios and transfers the power from the torque converter to the driveshaft(s).

_____3. Perform a preliminary stall test. Accelerate the engine to part (medium) throttle (for no more than 5 seconds) in each gear range to get a quick check for slippage of the apply devices. Enter "S" in the following chart to indicate any slip that was noticed.

Transmission operation depends on proper operation of the three major systems.

Preliminary Stall Test

R	OD	D	2	1

_____4. Drive the vehicle at various throttle openings as you check the quality of the upshifts and downshifts. Enter the code letters in the following charts for any faults to indicate the type of problem noticed.

Upshifts	1-2	2	2-3	3	3-4	4
Light Throttle						
Medium Throttle						
Wide-open Throttle						
Manual						
Torque Conv. Clutch						

Downshifts	4-3	3	3-2	2	2-1
Manual					
Engine Braking					
Full Throttle					
Part Throttle					
Coast					

Code: E = early, L = late, H = harsh, M = miss, N = noisy, S = slip, SO = soft

_____5. What is your recommendation based on your road test?

OK _____ NOT OK _____

If NOT OK, what should be done to correct the problem? _____

_____   _____

E 18, DIAGNOSE DRIVETRAIN NOISE, VIBRATION, HARSHNESS (NVH) CONCERNS

Meets NATEF Task: (A-9) Diagnose noise and vibration concerns; determine necessary action. (P-2)

Name_____ Date_____

Make/Model_____ Year_____ Instructor's OK _____

Note: Some NVH concerns are tire and wheel related. These can often be isolated by swapping the tires to different positions on the vehicle or swapping the tires with those on a known-good vehicle. Tire noise concerns usually produce different noise pitch or tone on different pavement types.

_____ 1. Road test the vehicle to verify the concern. Determine the nature of the problem, and the condition(s) at which it occurs.

Tip: Power train problems are often engine torque related. Torque related problems change intensity with throttle position and load. Excess gear train slack that causes a "clunk" on neutral to drive or reverse shifts also indicates a power train problem.

What is the type of concern? Noise _____ Vibration _____ Harshness _____

At what speed does the problem occur? Problem speed: _____

Under what driving conditions does the problem occur? Check any of the following that apply:

Steady speed _____ **Accelerating** _____ **Decelerating** _____ **Coasting** _____

While driving straight _____ **Turning right** _____ **Turning left** _____

Changes with different transmission gear ranges: _____

Changes with different road surfaces: _____

Tip: A noise or vibration problem that changes with different gear ranges indicates a probable transmission problem.
Tip: Final drive noises will usually increase in intensity as speed increases and as load changes.

_____ 2. Raise the vehicle, and have a helper start the engine and shift through the gear ranges as you observe the transmission, powertrain mounts, driveshaft, and exhaust system.

Caution: Be extremely careful as you get close to the rotating tires and driveshaft(s).
Tip: Excessive movement at the powertrain mounts indicate a faulty mount.

OK _____ NOT OK _____

_____ 3. If there is a noise or vibration problem that changes with the gear range, indicate which ranges are objectionable?

Neutral _____ 1ˢᵗ _____ 2ⁿᵈ _____ 3ʳᵈ _____ 4ᵗʰ _____ Reverse _____ Park _____

Tip: A torque converter problem is indicated if noise is heard in gear but not in park or neutral.
Tip: Pump and hydraulic noises occur in gear, park, and neutral. Hydraulic noise will increase if you force line pressure or TV pressure to increase.
Tip: Many transmissions have a 1:1 ratio in third gear; gear train noise problems normally occur in the other gear ranges because there is gear action.

_____ 3. Using service information, what apply devices (driving and reaction) are applied during the objectionable gear range?

Driving Member: _____

Reaction Member: _____

_____ 4. What components in the gear set are rotating and transferring power when the problem occurs?

Planetary Driven Member: _____

Planetary Held/Reaction Member: _____

Planetary Output Member: _____

_____ 5. What is the likely cause of the concern?

Cause: _____

_____

E 19, CHECK HYDRAULIC SYSTEM PRESSURES

Meets NATEF Task: (A-6 & 11) Perform pressure tests (including transmissions/transaxles equipped with electronic pressure control); determine necessary action. (P-1)

Name_____ Date_____

Make/Model_____ Year_____ Instructor's OK _____

_____1. Locate the procedures for checking the transmission fluid pressure

     Information source: _____ **Section:**_____ **Page:**_____

_____2. Locate each of the test ports, and determine the thread type used at each?

     Identify the available test ports:

     Number of ports: _____
     Line _____
     Governor _____   **2-4** _____
     Throttle _____   **2nd** _____
     Reverse _____   **4th** _____
     TCC On ____   **OD** ____
     TCC Off _____   **Low-Rev.** _____
     Drive _____   **Other:** _____

     Test port thread: 1/8" pipe _____ **1/4"** _____ **Other, Identify:** _____

_____3. Attach a pressure gauge to the line pressure port, and perform the pressure checks. Enter the pressure readings in the charts below.

Mechanical Throttle Valve and Electronic Transmission

Engine Speed	Throttle	Park	Neutral	Over-drive	Drive	Man. 1	Man. 2	Reverse
Idle	Closed							
1,000 rpm	Closed							
Idle	WOT							
1,000 rpm	WOT							

    Caution: Limit each 1,000 rpm test to 5 seconds maximum.
    Caution: If stall testing a transmission with electronic pressure control and the EPC disconnected, be aware that the transmission can be damaged by high torque transfer.

Vacuum Modulator Transmission

Engine Speed	Vacuum	Park	Neutral	Over-drive	Drive	Man. 1	Man. 2	Reverse
Idle	+ 15"Hg							
1,000 rpm	+ 15"Hg							
Idle	0" Hg							
1,000 rpm	0"Hg							

_____4. Compare your readings with the specifications. Are any of the pressure readings out of range?

Yes _____ **No** _____

If yes, which ones? _____

What do the bad pressure readings indicate?

_____

_____

_____

E 20, PERFORM A STALL TEST

Meets NATEF Task: (A-7) Perform stall test; determine necessary action. (P-1)

Name_____ Date_____

Make/Model_____ Year_____ Instructor's OK _____

Note: Follow each of these recommendations when performing a stall test.
- The engine and transmission should be at operating temperature.
- The vehicle tires must be blocked with the brakes firmly applied.
- Do not allow anyone to be in front of or behind the vehicle.
- Limit each test to a maximum of 5 seconds.
- Let vehicle run in neutral for several minutes between each of the checks.

_____1. Locate the stall test procedure for this vehicle.

Information source: _____ **Section:**_____ **Page:**_____

_____2. Use the tachometer in the
vehicle or connect a tachometer.

_____3. Place blocks in front of and
behind the drive wheels.

_____4. Firmly apply the parking and
service brakes. Shift the
transmission into the desired
gear range, open the throttle
completely, and observe the
tachometer. As soon as the rpm
stabilizes, release the throttle, and shift into park or neutral. Record the highest rpm for
each range in the chart.

*Tip: Use a grease pencil or
piece of tape to mark the
maximum rpm on the face of
the tachometer. Stop your test
immediately if the rpm
exceeds the maximum stall
speed specification.*

**This vehicle is in Drive,
WOT, and is stationary.**

The tachometer is showing a stall speed of about 2,300 rpm.

	Gear Range			
	Drive	Manual 1	Manual 2	Reverse
Stall RPM				
	OK _____ High _____ Low _____	OK _____ High _____ Low _____	OK _____ High _____ Low _____	OK _____ High _____ Low _____

_____5. Compare the stall rpm to the specification, and mark the appropriate condition in the chart.

> *Tip:* *Excess stall rpm indicates slippage inside the transmission.*
> *Tip:* *Low stall speeds indicate a torque converter or engine problem.*

_____6. Is there a problem with this vehicle?

Yes _____ No _____

If yes, what is your diagnosis ?

_____

_____

E 21, CHECK VACUUM MODULATOR OPERATION

Name_____ Date_____

Make/Model_____ Year_____ Instructor's OK _____

_____1. Locate and check the modulator vacuum hose, metal line, and the connection to the engine intake manifold.

     OK _____
     NOT OK _____

_____2. Locate and check the vacuum hose and its connection to the <u>vacuum modulator</u>.

     OK _____
     NOT OK _____

Vacuum Tube/Hose

Modulator

Downshift Cable

Tip: Wipe the inside of the vacuum hose using a pipe cleaner or Q-tip; a red ATF stain indicates a bad modulator diaphragm.

_____3. Attach a vacuum gauge to the vacuum hose. Run the engine at idle speed, and measure the vacuum.
     Tip: There should be a steady vacuum of 14--22"Hg (44-57 kPa).

     Specified Vacuum: _____ **Measured Vacuum:** _____

     OK _____ **NOT OK** _____

_____4. Disconnect the vacuum hose to create a leak; the engine should stall or run rough.

     OK _____ **NOT OK** _____

Vacuum Modulator

Vacuum Port

O-ring Seal

_____5. Remove the modulator.

Modulator Valve

_____6. Connect a vacuum pump to the modulator. Apply a vacuum of 15–20"Hg. The vacuum should hold for at least 30 seconds.

OK _____ **NOT OK** _____

_____7. Remove the throttle/modulator valve, and insert it into the end of the modulator. A round rod of the proper diameter can be used as a substitute. Push inward on the valve; the spring should compress with a smooth motion.

Tip: If the transmission shift quality or timing is not correct, check the line pressure to vacuum relationship or "weigh" the modulator as described in the textbook.

OK _____ **NOT OK** _____

_____8. If the modulator does not compress smoothly, check for a bent modulator stem.

Tip: Roll the modulator across a bench top; a bent stem is indicated if it wobbles up and down.

OK _____ **NOT OK** _____

_____9. Reinstall the throttle valve and modulator or replace the modulator with a new one if necessary.

E 22, AIR TEST TRANSMISSION

Meets NATEF Task: (A-6 & C-20) Perform pressure tests (including transmissions/transaxles equipped with electronic pressure control); determine necessary action. (P-1)

Name_____ Date_____

Make/Model_____Year_____ Instructor's OK _____

Note: Most hydraulic circuits can be operated by applying air pressure. An air test is performed to verify the cause of a transmission or valve body problem and as a quality control test after a transmission repair. Wet air checks are performed to determine the exact location of a leak or the rate of the leak.

Air Test:

_____1. Remove the oil pan and the valve body.

_____2. Determine which circuit needs to be tested, and locate the passage for that circuit. *Tip: Most manufacturers provide an illustration with the fluid passages labeled for identification.*

_____3. Regulate the air pressure to 30--50 psi. Place the tip of the air nozzle against the passage and apply air pressure. Identify and list the clutch and band names as they are checked.

Clutch 1: _____
OK _____ NOT OK _____
Clutch 2: _____
OK _____ NOT OK _____
Clutch 3: _____
OK _____ NOT OK _____
Clutch 4: _____
OK _____ NOT OK _____
Clutch 5: _____
OK _____ NOT OK _____
Band 1: _____
OK _____ NOT OK _____
Band 2: _____   OK _____ NOT OK _____
Band 3: _____   OK _____ NOT OK _____

Tip: An air nozzle with a rubber tip can be simply pressed against a round passage opening. Slotted passages can be covered with a shop cloth or test plate to prevent an air loss.

Tip: As you apply air pressure to the circuit, listen for escaping air or the sound of a clutch or servo piston applying. A clutch will make a dull thud or thunk sound when it applies. Air to the servo apply port will apply the band.

Tip: Escaping air inside the transmission indicates a leak; you can often follow the sound to locate the leak area. Knowledge of the internal operation of the transmissions is very helpful when conducting this test.

Wet Air Test:

_____4. Place a small amount of ATF into the circuit being tested and repeat the air test. Be prepared for a spray of ATF while testing and when the air nozzle is removed.

Tip: A pressure of 30--40 psi is recommended for this test.

Tip: Air pressure will force ATF through any leaks in the circuit, and this will show the location of the leak. The rate of leakage will give you an indication of the size of the leak.

OK _____ NOT OK _____

If not OK, where is the leak?

_____

_____

Regulator Apply
No Leakage Allowed

Spool Valve
No Leakage Allowed

Exhaust
No Leakage Allowed

E 23, TORQUE CONVERTER DIAGNOSIS

Meets NATEF Task: (A-8) Perform lock-up converter tests; determine necessary action. (P-1)

Name_____ Date_____

Make/Model_____ Year_____ Instructor's OK _____

Stator Clutch:

_____1. Drive the vehicle on a road test, and note torque converter operation.

      OK _____ **NOT OK** _____

> *Tip:* A freewheeling stator clutch will cause poor acceleration and a low stall speed.
> *Tip:* A locked stator clutch will cause limited/reduced engine RPM and vehicle speed because of the fluid drag; acceleration will be normal. Visual inspection may show that the converter has a blue color from overheating.
> *Tip:* Faulty turbine to input shaft splines and worn internal thrust washers will often show up during a stall test as unusual noises or a freewheeling engine.

Torque Converter Clutch (TCC):

_____2. Note the quality of TCC application during the road test.

      OK _____ **NOT OK** _____

RPM Drop/TCC Apply

> *Tip:* Normal TCC application causes the engine speed to drop 50--100 rpm. TCC release can cause a greater rpm change depending on throttle position. While the TCC is released, engine rpm can fluctuate with throttle changes. While the TCC is applied, engine rpm will only increase as vehicle speed increases.
> *Tip:* A shudder that occurs during TCC apply can be caused by improper or dirty fluid and worn lining or seals.
> *Tip:* A shudder that occurs after TCC apply is caused be something other than the transmission, usually an engine problem, worn powertrain mounts, or a faulty driveshaft.

OIL COOLER   PRESSURE GAUGE

_____3. If the TCC does not apply, connect a pressure gauge to the cooler line coming from the transmission (not the return line). Make sure that the pressure hose is away from the exhaust system and any moving parts. Road test the vehicle, and watch the pressure gauge for a pressure change.

Caution: Do not bring the pressure gauge into the passenger area. Some technicians tape the gauge to the outside of the windshield for easy viewing from the drivers seat.
Tip: A momentary pressure drop of 5 to 10 psi (35 – 70 kPa) indicates that the control system is functioning properly.

OK _____ **NOT OK** _____

Tip: No TCC apply with a functioning control system indicates a bad torque converter.

Flow Meter:

_____4. If a flow meter is available, connect the sensor and gauge to the cooler line. Monitor the cooler flow during a road test (see textbook Chapter 12).

OK _____ **NOT OK** _____

Electronic Control System:

_____5. Connect a scan tool to the vehicle diagnostic port. Depending on the vehicle and tool, check for TCC-related diagnostic trouble codes, DTCs, or the TCM command for the TCC to apply.

OK _____ **NOT OK** _____

_____6. Road test the vehicle. During the road test, use the scan tool to command TCC to apply, and check for actual TCC apply.

OK _____ **NOT OK** _____

NATEF

E 24, COOLER CIRCUIT FLUID FLOW

Name_____ **Date**_____

Make/Model_____ **Year**_____ **Instructor's OK** _____

Note: Cooler circuit checks require that the transmission fluid level be correct.

<u>**Simple Check:**</u>

_____1. Determine which line transfers fluid to the cooler and which line returns fluid to the transmission.

    Transmission out: _____

    Transmission Return: _____

_____2. Disconnect the cooler line coming from the transmission (not the return line) at the cooler connection. Attach a rubber hose to the line, and insert the other end of the hose into a container that has a 1 quart graduation.

    Tip: A graduation can be marked onto any container using a felt-tip marker.
    Tip: Be prepared for a strong fluid flow from the hose as soon as the engine starts.

_____2. Have a helper start the engine as you observe the fluid flow. After 20 seconds, shut the engine off.

    OK _____ **NOT OK** _____

    Tip: Normal cooler fluid flow is about 1 quart per 20 seconds.

_____3. If the a restricted cooler is suspected, reconnect the cooler line, and disconnect the cooler return line at the transmission. Repeat Steps 1 and 2.

    OK _____ **NOT OK** _____

    Tip: A lower flow than in Step 2 indicates a restricted cooler that should be flushed or replaced.

<u>**Cooler Flow Sensor:**</u>

_____4. Disconnect the cooler line at a convenient location, and connect the flow sensor in series with the cooler line.

_____5. Attach the display unit to the sensor, and connect it to the vehicle's power receptacle.

_____6. Start the engine, and read the flow rate on the display.

OK _____ **NOT OK** _____

Note: Some vehicle manufacturers provide cooler flow rate specifications.
Tip: As a rule of thumb, the cooler circuit should flow about 0.6 gallon per minute at idle speed.
Tip: If other problems are suspected, the vehicle can be road tested with the flow meter attached. Never bring a pressure gauge into the interior of the vehicle. Pressure loss in the transmission hydraulic circuit will cause a drop in cooler flow rate. Remember that certain pressure fluctuations such as a pressure drop during a shift are normal.

_____7. Inspect both lines and all their connections for fluid leaks.

OK _____ **NOT OK** _____

E 25, TEST ELECTRONIC CONTROLS

Meets NATEF Task: (B-3 & 4) Inspect, test, adjust, repair, or replace electrical/electronic components and circuits, including computers, solenoids, sensors, relays, terminals, connectors, switches, and harnesses. (P-1)

Name_____ **Date**_____

Make/Model_____ **Year**_____ **Instructor's OK** _____

_____1. Locate the manufacturer's recommended self-diagnosis procedure.

Information source: _____ **Section:** _____ **Page:** _

_____2. Which gear is used for limp-in/fail-safe operation?

Fail-safe gear: _____

_____3. Remove the transmission fuse(s) and road test the vehicle. Note any change in transmission operation.

Changes: None _____ **Yes, describe:** _____

Tip: With the fuse removed, the transmission will only operate in fail-safe mode. There should be normal operation in all ranges except Drive, and Drive should have only one forward gear: fail-safe. Any problems that appear at this time are not caused by the failure of an electronic component.

_____4. Indicate the operations that must be done to enter and read self-diagnosis.

Install jumper wire _____
Connect a voltmeter _____
Connect and manipulate scan tool _____

Scan Tool

_____5. Is the diagnostic trouble code (DTC) read from the malfunction indicator lamp (MIL)?

Yes _____ **NO** _____
If yes, are there any codes indicated by the MIL? Yes _____ **No** _____

If yes, what diagnostic trouble code (DTC) is indicated?

DTC: _____, **Description:** _____

DLC Cable

Note: Any codes should be cleared, and the system operated to determine if the DTC resets.

_____6. Operate the vehicle, and retrieve any new DTCs from the system. Were any codes set?

Yes _____, How many? _____, No _____

If yes, what diagnostic trouble code (DTC) is indicated?
A. DTC: _____, Description: _____
B. DTC: _____, Description: _____
C. DTC: _____, Description: _____

_____7. What vehicle problem can produce this DTC?
    A._____
    B._____
    C._____

_____8. Briefly describe the steps required to locate the cause of this DTC.

Note: If a system fault was found and repaired, you should retest the vehicle to confirm proper repair.

_____9. Briefly describe the steps required to clear the DTCs on this vehicle.

If you have access to a scan tool, connect it to the vehicle.

_____10. Many scan tools allow you to read the output from the various sensors. Can you read sensor output?

Yes _____ No _____, If yes, are the sensors operating properly? Yes _____ No _____

_____11. Many scan tools allow you to read the signal to the solenoids. Can you read solenoid signals?

Yes _____ No _____, If yes, are the signals operating properly? Yes _____ No _____

_____12. Many scan tools allow you to control transmission operation and apply the various solenoids.

Yes _____ No _____, If yes, are the solenoids operating properly? Yes _____ No _____

50

E 26, DIAGNOSE ELECTRONIC TRANSMISSION CONCERN

Meets NATEF Task: (B-3 & 4) Inspect, test, adjust, repair, or replace electrical/electronic components and circuits, including computers, solenoids, sensors, relays, terminals, connectors, switches, and harnesses. (P-1)

Name_____ Date_____

Make/Model_____ Year_____ Instructor's OK _____

Under-hood inspection:
_____1. Visually inspect electrical wiring and components.

Battery cables and terminals:	**OK** _____ **NOT OK** _____
Ground straps:	**OK** _____ **NOT OK** _____
Altered wiring:	**OK** _____ **NOT OK** _____
Transmission related wiring connections:	**OK** _____ **NOT OK** _____

Scan Tool:
_____2. Connect a scan tool, and check for diagnostic trouble codes (DTCs) with the key on and engine off.
  Tip: With the engine off, the scan tool will read any codes that are in the memory.

  Codes: _____

_____3. Connect the scan tool, and check for DTCs with the key on and engine running.

  Codes: _____

_____4. Clear the codes, and recheck to see if the codes come back.
  Tip: If the codes return immediately, they are either hard codes or the self-check has found a circuit problem.

  OK _____ **NOT OK** _____

Road Test:
_____5. Perform a road test with the scan tool or a signal monitor attached to the vehicle.
  Tip: The TCM monitors the electronic components, and any new codes will be set as the faulty component operates.

  OK _____ **NOT OK** _____ **If not OK, which codes were indicated?** _____
  DTC: _____ **Description:** _____
  Note: Codes should be cleared, and the system operated to determine if the DTC resets.

Under Vehicle Inspection:
_____6. Visually inspect the exterior transmission components, wiring, and oil pan.

Range sensor/switch: OK _____ NOT OK _____
Wiring harness: OK _____ NOT OK _____
Altered harness: OK _____ NOT OK _____
Harness connectors: OK _____ NOT OK _____
Speed sensors: OK _____ NOT OK _____
Pan damage: OK _____ NOT OK _____

Tip: A crushed oil pan can cause damage to the internal components.

Voltage Checks:
_____7. Set a voltmeter to the DC volts scale. Connect the leads to the battery terminals observing the proper polarity.

Battery Voltage
Engine off: _____ V, Cranking: _____ V, Running: _____ V

Tip: With the engine off, battery voltage should be 12--13 V. The voltage should not drop below 10.5 V with the engine cranking. After the engine starts, the alternator should increase the voltage to 13.5--15.5 V.

Voltage Drop Checks:
_____8. For the following checks, connect the positive voltmeter lead to the most positive point in the circuit and the negative lead to the most negative point. With the engine running, what are the meter readings?

Positive post of the Battery to TCM B+ Connector: _____ V
If used, Positive post of the Battery to Transmission Relay: _____ V
     Transmission Relay to Transmission B+ Connector: _____ V
TCM Ground Connector to Battery Ground: _____ V
Transmission Case to Battery Ground: _____ V

Tip: A voltage drop greater than 0.1 V per connection indicates a problem. Wiggle the wire connectors and tap the electrical components with a plastic screwdriver handle as you watch the meter reading.
Tip: Electronic components are affected by temperature. If the problem is not found, warm the vehicle to normal operating temperature, and repeat the checks.
Note: If a system fault was found and repaired, you should always retest the vehicle to confirm proper repair.
Tip: If the problem is not found, it is probably being caused by a faulty sensor signal or solenoid operation. Check to determine cause of the DTCs found in Step5.

E 27, REPAIR ELECTRICAL WIRE AND TERMINAL

Meets NATEF Task: (B-3 & 4) Inspect, test, adjust, repair, or replace electrical/electronic components and circuits, including computers, solenoids, sensors, relays, terminals, connectors, switches, and harnesses. (P-1)

Name_____ Date_____

Make/Model_____ Year_____ Instructor's OK _____

Note: Repairing a damaged wire or faulty terminal connector can save the expense of replacing a wire harness.

Wire Splice, Soldered:

_____1. Obtain a short section of electrical wire. Remove 3/8" (9.5 mm) of insulation from the end of each wire. Note the wire gauge as you use the stripping and crimping tool.

Wire Gauge: _____

_____2. Push the wire ends together so the strands overlap, and twist the strands slightly to hold them together.

Tip: If you are using shrink tube for insulation, install it before connecting the wire ends.
Tip: A splice clip can be placed over the joint to reinforce the connection.

_____3. Apply heat to the wire connection, and touch solder to the hot wire. It should melt and flow between the strands of wire.

Note: Only rosin core solder should be used for electrical repairs; never use acid core solder.

_____4. Insulate the connection by wrapping it tightly with plastic tape or heating shrink tube so it fits tightly over the splice.

Tip: Wrap the insulating tape at an angle of about 45 degrees to the wire. This will result in a tight, well insulated joint.
Tip: If using shrink tube, a water-tight seal can be obtained by putting a drop of Hot Melt Glue in each end of the tube before shrinking it..

_____5. Test your connection by trying to pull it apart; it should not separate.

OK _____ **NOT OK** _____

Wire Splice, Crimp Connector:

_____6. Obtain a short section of electrical wire and remove 3/8" (9.5 mm) of insulation from each. Note the wire gauge as you use the stripping and crimping tool.

Wire Gauge: _____

Wires inserted into connector

Crimped Connector

_____7. Place a crimp connector over the bared wire ends, and lock it in place using the proper crimping section of the stripping and crimping tool.

Insulation tube shrunk from heat

_____8. Test your connection by trying to pull it apart; it should not separate.

OK _____ NOT OK _____

Remove and Replace Connector Terminal:

_____9. Select a wire connector, locate the locking tab, and manipulate the locking tab to disconnect the connector.

_____10. Inspect the connector to locate terminal locking tab.

_____11. Obtain the proper tool, and push the locking tab inward as you pull the wire and terminal from the back of the connector.

Connector

_____12. Check the locking tab to insure that it is not bent or damaged, and slide the terminal back into the connector. Test your installation by trying to pull the wire back out; it should be locked in place.

Terminal Release Tool

OK _____ NOT OK _____

_____13. Replace the connector, making sure that the locks are completely engaged.

E 28, REMOVE FRONT WHEEL DRIVE (FWD) DRIVESHAFT

Name_____ Date_____

Make/Model_____ Year_____ Instructor's OK _____

_____ 1. Locate the recommended driveshaft removal procedure.

Information source: _____ **Section:** _____ **Page:** _

_____ 2. Shift the gear selector to Park or 1st gear, and firmly apply the parking brake. Remove the hub cap/wheel cover, and loosen the front hub nut(s).
Tip: Expect the hub nuts to be very tight.

_____ 3. Raise the vehicle so there is access to the driveshafts with the front wheels hanging down.

_____ 4. Complete the removal of the front hub nut.

_____ 5. Disconnect the lower ball joint, pry the control arm downward, and separate the steering knuckle from the control arm.
Tip: On some vehicles, the driveshaft can be removed through an opening in the steering knuckle.

_____ 6. Pull the outboard CV joint through the hub to separate them.
Note: A puller is sometimes required to force the CV joint out of hub.

_____ 7. Use a slide hammer with puller attachment or a pry bar to pop the inboard CV joint out of the transaxle.

Tip: Be ready to support the weight of the driveshaft when it is removed.

Tip: On some vehicles, the inboard CV joint is bolted to a flange coming from the transaxle.

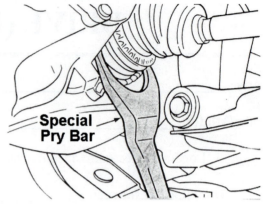

Tip: Try to keep the driveshaft in a horizontal position.

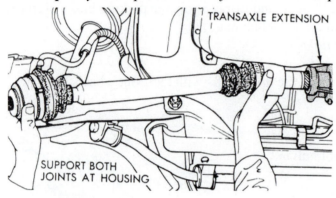

Tip: Do not lower the vehicles weight onto the front wheels with the driveshaft removed. The front wheel bearings can be damaged.

E 29, REPLACE FRONT WHEEL DRIVE (FWD) DRIVESHAFT

Name_____ Date_____

Make/Model_____ Year_____ Instructor's OK _____

_____ 1. Locate the recommended procedure for this operation.

Information source: _____ **Section:** _____, **Page:** _____

_____ 2. Raise the vehicle so there is access to the driveshaft with the front wheels hanging down.

_____ 3. Slide the inboard CV joint into transaxle as far as possible.
Tip: You should be able to feel or hear the circlip snap into place. Test the installation by trying to pull the CV joint back out; it should be locked in place.
Tip: A circlip that hangs downward can catch as the driveshaft is slid into the transaxle. Partially fill the circlip groove with transmission assembly grease to hold the circlip centered.
Tip: With some vehicles, the inboard CV joint is bolted to a flange coming from the transaxle.

Circlip   Differential Side Gear

Shaft is installed when circlip seats in groove   Groove

_____ 4. Pull the steering knuckle outward and guide the outboard CV joint through the hub to join them. Install a new hub nut and tighten it to pull the CV joint through the hub.
Tip: A puller is sometimes required to pull the CV joint through the hub.

_____ 5. Pry the control arm downward, and reconnect the control arm and lower ball joint to the steering knuckle. Tighten the retaining nut for the ball joint to the correct torque, and install the cotter pin if used.

Steering Knuckle

Lower Ball Joint

Install new ball joint attaching bolt and nut

_____ 6. Install the front hub nut and tighten it to pull the CV joint completely into the hub.
Tip: You will be unable to tighten the hub nut to the correct torque with the wheel in the air.

_____ 7. Lower the vehicle, shift the gear selector to Park or 1st gear, and firmly apply the parking brake. Tighten the hub nut to the correct torque, and lock the nut using the proper method.

_____ 8. Replace the front wheels, and tighten the lug nuts to the correct torque using a torque wrench.

Lug nut torque: _____

E 30, REMOVE AND REPLACE (R&R) REAR WHEEL DRIVE (RWD) DRIVESHAFT

Name_____ Date_____

Make/Model_____ Year_____ Instructor's OK _____

Note: Some driveshafts are bolted to flanges at both ends. On these vehicles, be prepared to suspend the first end of the shaft that is disconnected. **Do not** let the driveshaft hang from a single U-joint.

Remove:

_____ 1. Raise and securely support the vehicle so you have access to the driveshaft.

_____ 2. Place index marks on the rear axle flange and the rear U-joint/flange.

_____ 3. Remove the U-joint retaining bolts. Separate the U-joint from the flange, and slide the slip yoke out of the transmission.
Tip: Be prepared for a fluid spill from the back of the transmission. Use a drip pan or stop-off tool. An old driveshaft yoke makes a good stop-off tool.
Tip: Be prepared for the bearing caps to fall off of the rear joint. Secure the caps in place by wrapping a strip of tape around the joint.

U-joint

U-Bolt

Index Marks

Rear Axle
Companion Flange

Replace:

_____ 4. Lubricate the internal slip yoke splines with a special spline lubricant, and the outer slip portion with transmission fluid.
Tip: Dry splines can cause a binding with a "clunk" noise.

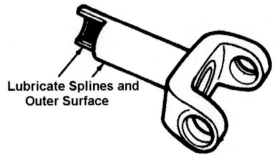

Lubricate Splines and
Outer Surface

_____ 5. Slide the slip yoke into the transmission, and position the rear U-joint in the rear axle flange.
Tip: *Make sure that the index marks are aligned and the bearing cups are seated properly in the flange.*

_____ 6. Replace the retaining bolts, and tighten them to the correct torque.

E 31, REMOVE, REPAIR, AND REPLACE GOVERNOR

Name_____ Date_____

Make/Model_____ Year_____ Instructor's OK _____

Note: The governor is mounted under a cover in General Motors transmissions. It is mounted inside the extension housing of many of the other RWD transmissions. Some transmissions require extensive disassembly to gain access to the governor.

Removal, GM:

_____1. Remove the retaining ring or bolts that secure the governor cover, and remove the cover.

_____2. Pull the governor out of the transmission; note that it must rotate as the drive gear comes out of mesh with the main shaft.

Removal, Others:

_____3. Remove the extension housing as described in Exercise 32.

_____4. Remove the bolts and/or retaining ring that secure the governor to the mainshaft.

Tip: Some transmissions use a key or steel ball to drive the governor; make sure that it does not get lost.

Repair:

_____5. Check the governor for these possible problems.

Sticking valve, primary: **OK _____ NOT OK _____**
            secondary: **OK _____ NOT OK _____**
Sticking or worn weight: **OK _____ NOT OK _____**
Worn or damaged drive gear: **OK _____ NOT OK _____**
Worn or damaged governor bore: **OK _____ NOT OK _____**

Tip: Some of these problems can be cured by cleaning the parts; serious problems require replacement.

Replace, GM:

_____6. Slide the governor into the transmission, making sure the drive gear aligns with the teeth of the mainshaft.

_____7. Install a new sealing O-ring or gasket, and replace the governor and the retaining ring or bolts. If bolts are used, tighten the bolts to the correct torque.

Bolt torque specification: _____

Tip: A C6 servo cover makes a very good installation tool for a stamped metal governor cover.

Replace, Others:

_____8. Slide the governor onto the mainshaft (making sure that the drive ball/key if used is in place). Install a new gasket if used.

_____9. Install the retaining ring and/or bolts, and tighten the mounting bolts to the correct torque.

Bolt torque specification: _____

_____ 10. Install the extension housing and described in Exercise 32. Torque the bolts to specifications.

Bolt torque specification: _____

E 32, REMOVE, AND REPLACE (R&R) EXTENSION HOUSING

Name_____ Date_____

Make/Model_____ Year_____ Instructor's OK _____

Note: The extension housing is removed to gain access to the governor and to facilitate replacement of the rear bushing, and seal.

Remove:

Index Marks

_____1. Raise the vehicle to gain access to the driveshaft(s) and transmission.

_____2. Place index marks on the rear U-joint and drive pinion shaft flange. This will ensure that the driveshaft is replaced in the original position.

_____3. Remove the driveshaft, being prepared for a fluid spill from the transmission.

Tip: Stop-off tools are available that can be inserted into the transmission to plug the leak. Some technicians use an old driveshaft slip joint for a transmission plug.

_____4. Remove the bolts that secure the transmission mount to the extension housing, and use a transmission jack to lift the transmission slightly off the mount.
Tip: Be careful not to crush the transmission pan with the jack.

_____5. Remove the bolts that secure the extension housing to the transmission, and remove the extension housing.
Tip: Some vehicles need the cross member/transmission support removed before the extension housing can be removed.
Tip: On some vehicles, the speedometer-driven gear must be removed to allow removal of the extension housing.
Tip: The speedometer drive gear is often held on the output shaft by a spring clip or snap ring.

Replace:

_____6. Place a new gasket/O-ring seal in position, and then place the extension housing in position on the transmission.
   Tip: Inspect the speedometer or speed sensor before replacing the extension housing,

_____7. Install the extension housing retaining ring and/or bolts, and tighten the mounting bolts to the correct torque.

   Bolt torque specification: _____

_____8. Install the transmission mount bolts, and tighten the mounting bolts to the correct torque. Remove the support jack.

   Bolt torque specification: _____

_____9. Align the U-joint match marks, and install the driveshaft. Tighten the U-joint mounting bolts to the correct torque.

   Bolt torque specification: _____

E 33, REMOVE, AND REPLACE (R&R)
EXTENSION HOUSING BUSHING

Meets NATEF Task: (C-13) Inspect, bushings; determine necessary action. (P-2)

Name_____ **Date**_____

Make/Model_____**Year**_____ **Instructor's OK** _____

Note: Bushings should be checked for excessive wear or damage, and worn bushings should be removed and replaced.

Note: The extension housing is normally removed to gain access to the rear bushing or governor. The extension housing seal will also need to be replaced at this time.

Removal:

_____1. Remove the driveshaft and extension housing as described in Exercise 32. *Tip: Special tools are available for some transmissions that allow bushing and seal replacement with the extension housing in place.*

EXTENSION HOUSING   **EXTENSION HOUSING BUSHING REMOVAL TOOL**

_____2. Check the housing to determine the best bushing removal method. Also determine if the bushing should be driven into the housing or if it should be driven outward from the inside the extension housing.

Tip: Several bushing removal and replacement methods are described in Chapter 17.

Tip: Before removing the bushing, identify any fluid passages. Mark the housing so the new bushing can be installed in the same position.

TOOL HANDLE   **TOOL HANDLE**

REMOVING HEAD   **INSTALLING HEAD**

FRONT CLUTCH DRUM   **FRONT CLUTCH DRUM**   **BUSHING**

_____3. Remove the bushing by pulling or driving it out of the extension housing. *Tip: The illustration shows the removal and replacement of a clutch housing bushing; the procedure is essentially the same as other transmission bushings.*

REMOVAL   **INSTALLATION**

Replace:

_____4. Check the bushing and housing for oil feed passages that must be aligned during installation or other features that require precise bushing placement.
Tip: Some bushings have an oil feed hole that must be aligned with the passage in the bushing bore.

_____5. Press the new bushing into the housing.
Tip: Some bushings or housings must be staked to lock the bushing in place. Other bushings should be installed using a locking compound.

_____6. Replace all parts removed during Step 1, and tighten the mounting bolts to the correct torque.

Bolt torque specification: _____

E 34, REMOVE, AND REPLACE (R&R) METAL-BACKED SEAL

Meets NATEF Task: (B-2) Inspect and replace external seals, gaskets, and bushings. (P-2)

Name_____ **Date**_____

Make/Model_____ **Year**_____ **Instructor's OK** _____

Note: Most metal-backed seals are removed and replaced using similar procedures.

Remove:

Seal to be replaced: _____

_____1. Locate the manufacturer's recommend procedure to remove and replace this seal.

      Information source: _____
      Section: _____ **Page:** _____

Tip: Special tools are available for some transmissions that allow the extension housing bushing and seal to be replaced with the extension housing in place.

_____2. Remove the parts (manual shift lever, driveshaft) as needed to gain access to the seal.

      Tip: Several seal removal and replacement methods are described in text Chapter 14.

_____3. Remove the seal by pulling or driving it out of the housing.

Tip: This illustration shows the removal and replacement of an extension housing seal.

Replace:

_____4. Check the seal and housing for features that require precise seal placement.
      Tip: If the seal does not have a special sealant coating on the outside, most sources recommend applying a sealant around the seal shell to prevent leaks between the shell and case.

Tip: Check the surface that the seal lip rides on; if it is not clean and smooth, the new seal will leak. In some cases, a thin sleeve can be placed over a damaged sealing surface.

_____5. Press or drive the new seal into the housing.
   Tip: The driving tool must fit the seal shell evenly and completely to prevent damage to the shell.
   Tip: If driving the seal in place, the hammer blows can dislodge the garter spring. To prevent this, fill the seal cavity with petroleum jelly or transmission assembly lube to hold the spring in position.

_____6. Replace all parts removed during Step 2. Tighten any mounting/attaching bolts to the correct torque.

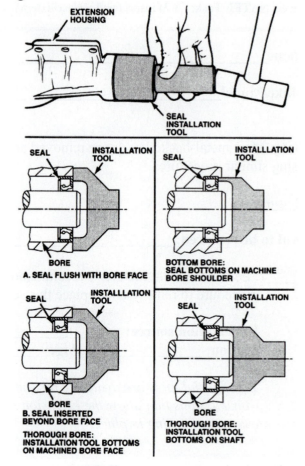

E 35, REMOVE, REPLACE, AND ALIGN POWERTRAIN MOUNTS

Meets NATEF Task: (B-5) Inspect, replace, and align powertrain mounts. (P-2)

Name_____ Date_____

Make/Model_____ Year_____ Instructor's OK _____

Note: Faulty mounts, also called insulators, will often show up as excessive engine movement during a stall test or noise on acceleration.

Inspection:

_____1. Visually check each mount and try to pry them apart as you look for the following problems.

Rubber breakup:	OK _____	NOT OK _____
Oil soaked:	OK _____	NOT OK _____
Separation:	OK _____	NOT OK _____
Other:	OK _____	NOT OK _____ Explain _____

Replacement:

_____2. Disconnect the negative battery cable. Raise the vehicle, and support the engine/transmission.

_____3. Remove the bolts connecting the mount to the engine/transmission, and slightly raise the engine/transmission so there is a clearance.
Tip: A support bracket is used along with the mount on some vehicles.

_____4. Remove the remaining bolts and the old mount.

_____5. Place the new mount in position, loosely install the bolts, lower the engine/transmission, and tighten the bolts to the correct torque.

Bolt torque specification: _____

Alignment:

Note: Neither the engine nor transmission should contact the vehicle body or frame. FWD vehicles should have the engine and transaxle centered so both of the inner CV joints have the same amount of in and out travel.

_____6. With the vehicle raised, compress one inner CV joint to make it as short as possible, and measure the distance between the CV joint body and the transmission.

Transaxle should be centered between CV joints

Measurement: _____

_____7. Repeat Step 6 at the other CV joint, and compare the two measurements.
Tip: The two measurements should be within 1/8 inch (5 mm).

Measurements: _____ **and** _____

Are the both equal? OK _____ **NOT OK** _____ **Difference:** _____

_____8. If there is a difference between the measurements, check the powertrain mounts to determine if both sides have slotted, adjustable mount holes. Loosen one or both mounts, and pry the engine/transmission so it will be centered.

_____9. Tighten the mounting bolts to the correct torque.

Torque specification: _____

E 36, INSTALL A THREAD INSERT

Name_____ Date_____

Make/Model_____ Year_____ Instructor's OK _____

Note: The female threads in aluminum castings are easily damaged (A). The casting can be saved by installing thread inserts to replace the damaged threads (B). Inserts resemble a small spring (C).

_____1. Locate the manufacturer's recommend procedure to prepare the casting and install the thread insert.

Thread to be repaired: _____
_____

Thread size: _____

Information source: _____ **Section:** _____ **Page:** _____

_____2. Remove the parts as needed to gain access to the damaged thread.
Tip: Many inserts require a three step procedure: A. Remove the old threads using a drill Bit; B. Cut new threads into the casting; and C. Install the insert.

_____3. Using a drill motor and drill bit of the specified size, carefully drill straight into the casting to remove the damaged threads.
Tip: The drill bit must follow the direction of the old threads.

A. **B.** **C.**

_____4. Using the proper tap and required lubricant, cut new threads into the casting.
Tip: The tap must be started straight in the hole.
Tip: Turn the tap backwards every half turn or so to break the metal chip so it can fall out of the tap.

_____5. Clean the metal chips from the hole.

_____6. Install the thread insert using the proper installation tool. If required, break off the insert tang.

_____7. Screw the bolt into the new threads. It should thread in easily.

OK _____ NOT OK _____

E 37, CLEAN TRANSMISSION COOLER

Meets NATEF Task: (C-6) Inspect, leak test, and flush or replace transmission/transaxle oil cooler, lines, and fittings. (P-1)

Name_____**Date**_____

Make/Model_____**Year**_____ **Instructor's OK** _____

Note: A transmission cooler can become plugged with debris from the torque converter. If this occurs, the transmission's lubrication flow will stop and serious transmission wear will occur.

_____1. Check cooler circuit flow as described in Exercise 24.

Tip: If the amount of flow is insufficient, the cooler will need to be flushed or replaced.

_____2. Disconnect both cooler lines at the most convenient location.

Tip: Use two flare-nut wrenches to remove the cooler line fittings: one to hold the connector and the other to turn the nut. Failure to do this can result in damage to the cooler lines.

Tip: Some vehicles use a quick-disconnect style of coupling at the cooler.

_____3. Attach the flushing unit to the <u>Fluid Out</u> side of the cooler using special adapters if needed.

Tip: The cooler should be flushed in both directions to remove as much debris as possible.

_____4. Attach a rubber hose to the <u>Fluid In</u> side of the cooler, and place the other end of this hose in a catch container.

Tip: *Some technicians use a coffee filter at the return hose to catch the debris coming out of the cooler. This allows them to inspect what comes out and to determine when the cooler becomes clean.*

_____5. Run the flushing material through the cooler until the return flow is clean.

_____6. Repeat Step 1 to insure a clean cooler.

_____7. When you are satisfied that the cooler is clean, reattach the cooler lines.

E 38, REMOVE AND REPLACE (R&R) VALVE BODY

Meets NATEF Task: (C-3) Inspect, measure, clean, and replace valve body (includes surfaces, bores, springs, valves, sleeves, retainers, brackets, check-valves/balls, screens, spacers, and gaskets). (P-2)

Name_____ Date_____

Make/Model_____ Year_____ Instructor's OK _____

Note: The valve body is removed for repair (E 48), valve body replacement, replacement of solenoids, or to replace the transfer plate and gaskets. It is recommended that both the transmission case and valve body are cool before removal.

Removal:

_____1. Disconnect the negative battery cable. Raise the vehicle as needed to gain access to the transmission.

_____2. Remove the fluid and pan as described in Exercise 7.
Tip: On some transaxles, the side pan is removed for access to the valve body.

_____3. Disconnect all wires and fluid transfer tubes connected to the valve body.
Tip: Some fluid transfer tubes may lift out of the case as the valve body is removed.
Tip: Be prepared for a fluid spill as the transfer tubes are removed and the valve body is loosened.

_____4. Remove the valve body retaining bolts.
Tip: The bolts may be different lengths. Note the location of the different bolts as they are removed.

_____5. Remove the valve body, gaskets and transfer plate.
Tip: Be prepared for check balls, filter screens, and springs to be released.

Replacement:

Note: *A used valve body and transfer plate should be inspected as described in Exercise 48.*

_____6. Compare the new gasket(s) with the old one(s) to insure the proper replacement, and place the gasket(s) and transfer plate in position on the valve body.
   Tip: *Check balls can be held in place with assembly lubricant or petroleum jelly.*

_____7. Place the valve body in position, and install the retaining bolts.
   Tip: *Two alignment pins threaded into the transmission case will help insure proper alignment of the gasket(s), transfer plate, and valve body.*
   Tip: *Make sure that the right length bolts go into the correct holes. Each bolt should thread into the case about 3/8 in. (9 mm).*

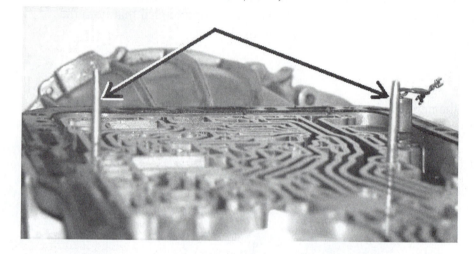

_____8. Replace all wire connections and fluid transfer tubes removed in Step 3.

_____9. Tighten the mounting bolts to the correct torque.

   Bolt torque specification: _____

_____10. Install a new filter, and replace the oil pan as described in E 7.

_____11. Fill the transmission with fluid, and replace the battery cable.

_____12. Start the engine, and shift through the gear ranges. Recheck the fluid level.

   OK _____ Low _____ High _____

E 41, REPLACE REAR WHEEL DRIVE (RWD) TRANSMISSION

Meets NATEF Task: (C-1) Remove and reinstall transmission/transaxle and torque converter; inspect engine core plugs, rear crankshaft seal, dowel pins, dowel pin holes, and mating surfaces. (P-1)

Name_____ Date_____

Make/Model_____ Year_____ Instructor's OK _____

_____ 1. Identify the transmission and its lubricant.

Transmission make: _____ **Model:** _____

Lubricant type: _____ **Level:** _____

_____ 2. Locate the manufacturer's transmission installation procedure.

Information source: _____ **Section:** _____, **Date:** _____

_____ 3. Raise and securely support the vehicle.
Tip: Check the flexplate for cracks.
Tip: It the converter has been replaced, check that the converter pilot fits into the crankshaft recess snugly but without binding.

_____ 4. Install the torque converter.
Tip: Make sure that it is installed completely. It needs to engage the reaction shaft, pump, and turbine. As a rule of thumb, the torque converter should be about one inch back from the front of the bell housing.

_____ 5. Place the transmission onto a transmission jack and adjust the supports and retaining chain so it is secure. Raise the transmission to the proper height.
Tip: Check that all transmission alignment dowel pins are in place.

_____ 6. Install one or two guide pins, place the transmission on the guide pins, and slide it into place. Install the transmission bolts, and tighten them to the correct torque.
Tip: The guide pins support much of the transmission's weight as they guide it into place.
Tip: There should be a slight clearance between the torque converter and flexplate when the transmission is completely installed.

Tip: Make sure that no wires, hoses, and linkages are caught between the transmission and the engine.

_____ 7. Raise the jack, if necessary, to lift the engine and transmission so the transmission support can be installed. Tighten the support bolts to the correct torque.

_____ 8. Replace the transmission mount, tighten the bolts to the correct torque, and remove the support jack.

_____ 9. Slide the torque converter forward, install the torque converter to flexplate fasteners, and tighten them to the correct torque. Replace the torque converter cover, and tighten the bolts to the correct torque.
Tip: If the converter bolts are too long because they have been replaced or the converter pads have been machined, they can bend the converter cover and cause converter clutch problems.

_____ 10. Replace all remaining connections between the transmission and the vehicle, such as the cooler lines, VSS/speedometer cable, electrical connections, and shift linkage.

_____ 11. Place a light coating of the proper grease on the output shaft splines and the driveshaft slip yoke, and slide the drive shaft slip yoke into the transmission. Align the index marks on the rear U-joint and drive axle flange, and reconnect the drive shaft to the axle.

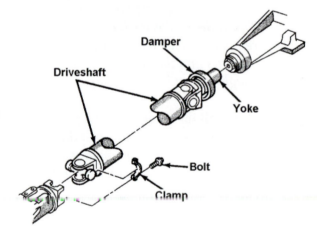

_____ 11. Confirm that you have the correct fluid, and fill the transmission to the proper level (E 6).
Tip: Make sure that the cooler lines, wires, and hoses are properly routed.

_____ 12. Make sure the ignition switch is turned off, and reconnect the battery. Start the engine, and check for proper transmission operation with no fluid leaks.

E 42, REPLACE FRONT WHEEL DRIVE (FWD) TRANSAXLE

Meets NATEF Task: (C-1) Remove and reinstall transmission/transaxle and torque converter; inspect engine core plugs, rear crankshaft seal, dowel pins, dowel pin holes, and mating surfaces. (P-1)

Name_____ Date_____

Make/Model_____ Year_____ Instructor's OK _____

_____ 1. Identify the transaxle and its lubricant.

Transaxle make: _____ **Model:** _____

Lubricant type: _____ **Level:** _____

_____ 2. Locate the manufacturer's installation procedure for the transaxle.

Information source: _____ **Section:** _____ **Date:** _

_____ 3. Raise and securely support the vehicle so there is access to the engine and front suspension.
Tip: Check the flexplate for cracks.
Tip: It the converter has been replaced, check that the converter pilot fits into the crankshaft recess snugly but without binding.

_____ 4. Install the torque converter.
Tip: Make sure that it completely engages the reaction shaft, pump, and turbine. As a rule of thumb, the torque converter should be about one inch back from the front of the bell housing.

_____ 5. Place the transaxle onto a transmission jack, and adjust the supports and retaining chain so it is secure. Raise the transaxle to the proper height.
Tip: Check that all transmission alignment dowel pins are in place.

_____ 6. Install one or two guide pins, place the transaxle onto the guide pins, and slide it into place. Install the bolts, and tighten them to the correct torque.
Tip: The guide pins support much of the transmission's weight as they guide it into place.
Tip: After the transmission is fully installed, there should be a slight clearance between the torque converter and flexplate.

Tip: Make sure that no wires, hoses, and linkages are caught between the transmission and the engine.

_____ 7. Install the transaxle support, and tighten the bolts to the correct torque.

_____ 8. Replace the transaxle mount(s), tighten the bolts to the correct torque, and remove the support jack/fixture.
Tip: The engine and transaxle position might need to be realigned (E 32).

_____ 9. Install the torque converter to flexplate bolts, and tighten them to the correct torque. Replace the torque converter cover, and tighten the bolts to the correct torque.
Tip: If the converter bolts are too long because they have been replaced or the converter pads have been machined, they can bend the converter cover and cause converter clutch problems.

_____ 10. Replace all connections under the vehicle between the transaxle and the vehicle, such as the cooler lines, VSS/speedometer cable, electrical connections, and shift linkage.

_____ 11. Place a light coating of the proper grease on the driveshaft splines, and slide the drive shafts into the transaxle. Slide the outboard CV joint through the hub, and reconnect the CV joint to the hub.
Tip: Test the connection of the inboard CV joint to the transaxle. You can often feel or hear the circlip engage, and you should not be able to pull the CV joint out of the transaxle.

_____ 12. Replace any suspension components that were disconnected or removed during transaxle removal.

_____ 13. Fill the transaxle with the correct lubricant to the proper level (E 6).

_____ 14. Lower the vehicle, tighten the front hub nuts to the correct torque, and install any locking device.

_____ 15. Remove the engine support.

_____ 16. Replace all remaining connections under the hood that were disconnected during removal like the cooler lines, VSS/speedometer cable, electrical connections, and shift linkage.
Tip: Make sure that the cooler lines, wires, and hoses are properly routed.

_____ 12. Make sure the ignition switch is turned off, and reconnect the battery. Start the engine, and check for proper transmission operation with no fluid leaks.

E 43, DISASSEMBLE REAR WHEEL DRIVE (RWD) TRANSMISSION

Meets NATEF Task: (C-2) Disassemble clean, and inspect transmission/transaxle. (P-1)

Name_____ Date_____

Make/Model_____ Year_____ Instructor's OK _____

Note: Automatic transmissions are normally disassembled by removing the major components, and then each component is serviced separately (disassembled, inspected, and reassembled using new parts as needed).

_____ 1. Identify the transmission.

   Transmission make: _____
   Model: _____

_____ 2. Locate the manufacturer's transmission disassembly procedure.

   Information source: _____
   Section: _____
   Page: _____

_____ 3. Locate and list all end play, clutch, and band clearance/servo stroke checks required by the manufacturer.
   Checks:

   _____
   _____
   _____
   _____
   _____
   _____

_____ 4. Preclean the transmission exterior to remove excessive dirt, oil, and grease.
   Tip: External debris will make the work area dirty; it can also confuse inspection of the internal parts if they pick up this debris.

_____ 5. Mount the transmission on a support fixture; you should be able to rotate the transmission so either the front, bottom, or rear end is up.

_____ 6. Remove the pan, and drain any remaining oil. Inspect the pan, magnet, and oil for metal or plastic particles that might be indicators of internal damage.

_____ 7. Position the transmission with the front upward, attach a dial indicator as described in textbook Chapter 16, and measure turbine shaft end play.
Tip: Excessive end play indicates worn thrust washers.

Measured end play: _____ **Specified end play:** _____

_____ 8. Disassemble the transmission following the procedure recommended by the manufacturer and described in text Chapter 16.
Caution: Some servos and accumulators have a strong internal spring. Watch the cover to see if it starts to lift up as you remove the bolts/retainer, and be sure to use the recommend tool during disassembly.
Tip: Check each component as it is removed to note how it came apart; this will make it easier to replace in the proper location. Many technicians will place index marks on the parts using a permanent marker or small die grinder to identify the location or position.
Tip: Before removing a one-way clutch, note the directions of locked and free rotation.

_____ 9. Perform all end play and band clearance/servo stroke checks as required by the manufacturer. List the checks that are required by the manufacturer.
Tip: Band/servo travel checks are often adjusted by using selective parts during reassembly.

Checks:

_____ OK _____ NOT OK _____
_____ OK _____ NOT OK _____
_____ OK _____ NOT OK _____
_____ OK _____ NOT OK _____
_____ OK _____ NOT OK _____
_____ OK _____ NOT OK _____

_____ 10. Perform a preliminary inspection of the major components as they are removed. Identify the clutches and bands as they are removed from the transmission.

Major Components:
Valve Body: OK _____ NOT OK _____
Front Pump: OK _____ NOT OK _____
_____ **Clutch: OK _____ NOT OK _____**
_____ **Clutch: OK _____ NOT OK _____**
_____ **Clutch: OK _____ NOT OK _____**
_____ **Clutch: OK _____ NOT OK _____**
_____ **Clutch: OK _____ NOT OK _____**
_____ **Clutch: OK _____ NOT OK _____**
_____ **Band: OK _____ NOT OK _____**
_____ **Band: OK _____ NOT OK _____**
_____ **Band: OK _____ NOT OK _____**
Planetary Gear Set: OK _____ NOT OK _____

E 44, DISASSEMBLE FRONT WHEEL DRIVE (FWD) TRANSAXLE

Meets NATEF Task: (C-2) Disassemble clean, and inspect transmission/transaxle. (P-1)

Name_____ Date_____

Make/Model_____ Year_____ Instructor's OK _____

Note: Automatic transaxles are normally disassembled by removing the major components, and then each component is serviced separately (disassembled, inspected, and reassembled using new parts as needed).

_____ 1. Identify the transaxle.

Transaxle make: _____
Model: _____

_____ 2. Locate the manufacturer's transaxle disassembly procedure.

Information source: _____
Section: _____
Page: _____

_____ 3. Locate and list all end play, clutch, and band clearance/servo stroke checks required by the manufacturer.
Checks:

_____
_____
_____
_____
_____
_____

_____ 4. Preclean the transaxle exterior to remove the excessive dirt, oil, and grease.
Tip: External debris will make the work area dirty; it can also confuse inspection of the internal parts if they pick up this debris.

_____ 5. Mount the transaxle on a support fixture; you should be able to rotate the transaxle for easy access to the front, bottom, or the ends.

_____ 6. Remove the pan, and drain out any remaining oil. Inspect the pan, magnet, and oil for metal or plastic particles that might be indicators of internal damage.

_____ 7. Position the transaxle as necessary, attach a dial indicator as described in textbook Chapter 16, and measure turbine shaft end play.

Tip: Excessive end play indicates worn thrust washers.

Measured end play: _____ **Specified end play:** _____

_____ 8. Disassemble the transaxle following the procedure recommended by the manufacturer and described in text Chapter 16.

Caution: Some servos and accumulators have a strong internal spring. Watch the cover to see if it starts to lift up as you remove the bolts/retainer, and be sure to use the recommend tool during disassembly.

Tip: Check each component as it is removed to note how it came apart. This step will make it easier to reinstall the parts in the proper location. Many technicians will place index marks on the parts using a permanent marker or small die grinder to show the location or position.

Tip: Before removing a one-way clutch, note the directions of locked and free rotation.

_____ 9. Perform all end play and band clearance/servo stroke checks as required by the manufacturer. List the checks that are required by the manufacturer.

Tip: Band/servo travel checks are often adjusted by using selective parts during reassembly.

Checks:

_____	OK _____	NOT OK _____
_____	OK _____	NOT OK _____
_____	OK _____	NOT OK _____
_____	OK _____	NOT OK _____
_____	OK _____	NOT OK _____
_____	OK _____	NOT OK _____

_____ 10. Perform a preliminary inspection of the major components as they are removed. Identify the clutches and bands as they are removed from the transmission.

Major Components:

Valve Body: OK _____ **NOT OK** _____

Front Pump: OK _____ **NOT OK** _____

_____ **Clutch: OK** _____ **NOT OK** _____

_____ **Clutch: OK** _____ **NOT OK** _____

_____ **Clutch: OK** _____ **NOT OK** _____

_____ **Clutch: OK** _____ **NOT OK** _____

_____ **Clutch: OK** _____ **NOT OK** _____

_____ **Clutch: OK** _____ **NOT OK** _____

_____ **Band: OK** _____ **NOT OK** _____

_____ **Band: OK** _____ **NOT OK** _____

_____ **Band: OK** _____ **NOT OK** _____

Planetary Gear Set: OK _____ **NOT OK** _____

E 45, DISASSEMBLE, INSPECT AND REASSEMBLE PUMP

Meets NATEF Task: (C-9) Inspect, measure, and reseal oil pump assembly and components. (P-1)

Name_____ Date_____

Make/Model_____ Year_____ Instructor's OK _____

Note: The major components are normally serviced separately. They are disassembled, inspected, and reassembled using new or reconditioned parts as needed.

_____ 1. Identify the transmission.

Transmission make: _____ **Model:** _____

_____ 2. Locate the manufacturer's inspection and repair procedure. Pump service is described in text Chapter 18.

Information source: _____ **Section:** _____ **Date:** _

_____ 3. Identify the type of pump used in this transmission.

**Pump Type: I-X Gear: _____, Gerotor: _____
Vane: _____**

_____ 4. Remove the bolts, and separate the pump cover from the body. Before removing the gears check for any location marks of the gears. Thoroughly clean the parts and visually inspect the parts for wear and scoring. *Tip: Some pump gears can be turned upside down, but if one gear is inverted, both gears should be inverted. Some gears have marks to show their position.*

Visual Inspection: OK _____ NOT OK _____

_____ 5. Perform the clearance checks as required by the manufacturer. List any additional checks required.

**A. Gear tip clearance
Measured:** _____
Specification: _____

OPTIONAL
IDENTIFICATION
MARKS

INNER
GEAR

FEELER
GAUGE

OUTER
GEAR

PUMP
BODY

MEASURE CLEARANCES
AT CRESCENT HERE

B. Gear/vane side clearance,
Measured: _____
Specification: _____

C. _____
Measured: _____
Specification: _____

D. _____
Measured: _____
Specification: _____

_____ 6. Check the body and cover bushings for wear.
Tip: Damaged or oversized bushings should be replaced.

Visual check: OK _____ **NOT OK** _____
Body bushing ID, Measured: _____ **Specification:** _____
Stator shaft bushing, Measured: _____ **Specification:** _____

_____ 7. Remove and replace the body and cover bushings if necessary.

Replaced bushings? Yes _____ **No** _____

_____ 8. Remove and replace the front seal. Check the drain back hole in the seal cavity.

Replaced seal? Yes _____ **No** _____
Drain back hole: OK _____ **NOT OK** _____

_____ 9. Lubricate the moving parts using assembly grease, petroleum jelly, or ATF, and assemble the pump.
Tip: If the body and cover have the same outside diameter, the outer diameter of the two parts must be aligned so they will not damage the case when the pump is installed.
Tip: Some manufacturers require a special alignment tool to properly align the pump gears during assembly. Technicians assemble the pump on a torque converter if the special tool is not available.

_____ 10. Install the bolts, and tighten them to the correct torque.
Tip: After the pump bolts have been tightened, place the pump on a torque converter, check that the bushing fit properly and then rotate the pump body to make sure the pumping member turn smoothly.

Bolt torque specification: _____

FEELER GAUGE

INNER ROTOR

OUTER ROTOR

E 46, DISASSEMBLE, INSPECT, AND REASSEMBLE CLUTCH

Meets NATEF Task: (C-18) Inspect clutch drum, piston, check-balls, springs, retainers, seals, and friction and pressure plates; determine necessary action. (P-2)

Name_____ Date_____

Make/Model_____ Year_____ Instructor's OK _____

Note: the major components of an automatic transmission are normally serviced separately. They are disassembled, inspected, and reassembled using new or reconditioned parts as needed.

_____ 1. Identify the transmission.

Transmission make:

_____

Model: _____

_____ 2. Locate the manufacturer's clutch repair procedure.
Tip: Clutch service is described in textbook Chapter 18.
Tip: Place the clutch friction discs in ATF now for later assembly.

Information source: _____ **Section:** _____ **Date:** _

_____ 3. Remove the retaining ring, and separate the clutch plates from the body. Clean the plates, and visually inspect the parts for wear.
Tip: If the transmission is being rebuilt, it is often required that the friction and steel plates be replaced with new ones.

OK _____ NOT OK _____
Number of friction plates: _____
steel plates: _____

_____ 4. Compress the clutch return springs, and remove the retaining ring, spring and clutch piston. Thoroughly clean the parts and visually inspect them for wear and damage.
Tip: The piston seals should be replaced. Note the direction of the seal lip as they are removed and replaced.
Tip: With stamped steel pistons and clutch housings, carefully inspect the welds for cracks and separation.

Housing: OK _____ NOT OK _____, Piston: OK _____ NOT OK _____

_____ 5. Check the housing thrust surfaces and bushings (if used) for wear.
Tip: Damaged, worn, or oversized bushings should be replaced.

Visual check: OK _____ **NOT OK** _____
Bushing ID, Measured: _____ **Specification:** _____

_____ 6. On rotating clutches, locate and check the check ball; it should move and rattle when you shake the piston/housing. Air check the ball to test for proper sealing.
Tip: The check ball should prevent an air flow from inside the clutch to the outside but allow an air flow from outside to inside.

Free movement: OK _____ **NOT OK** _____
Air check: OK _____ **NOT OK** _____

_____ 7. Install new seals on the piston, lubricate the seals using assembly grease, and assemble the piston into the clutch housing.
Tip: Carefully guide the piston seals into the housing as the piston is installed.

_____ 8. Install the return springs, and carefully compress them. Install the retaining ring, and carefully release the spring compressor. Check to make sure that the retaining ring is properly seated.

OK _____ **NOT OK** _____

_____ 9. Install the ATF soaked clutch discs into the clutch housing. Make sure that they are stacked in the correct order with the proper side up.

Number of frictions: _____
Steels: _____

_____ 10. Install the top pressure plate and retaining ring. Measure the clutch pack clearance, and adjust the clearance if necessary.
Tip: Pack clearance can be measured using a dial indicator. This test indicates the total clutch piston travel.

Clutch pack clearance
Measured: _____
Specification: _____

_____ 11. Air check the clutch to insure that it applies and releases properly (E 22).

OK _____ **NOT OK** _____

E 47, DISASSEMBLE, INSPECT, AND REASSEMBLE PLANETARY GEARSET

Meets NATEF Task: (C-14) Inspect and measure planetary gear assembly (includes sun, ring gear, thrust washers, planetary gears, and carrier assembly); determine necessary action. (P-2)

Name_____ **Date**_____

Make/Model_____ **Year**_____ **Instructor's OK** _____

Note: The major components of an automatic transmission are normally serviced separately. They are disassembled, inspected, and reassembled using new or reconditioned parts as needed.

_____ 1. Identify the transmission.

Transmission make:

_____

Model: _____

_____ 2. Locate the manufacturer's planetary gearset repair procedure.
Tip: Gearset service is described in textbook Chapter 18.

Information source: _____ **Section:** _____ **Page:** _

Gearset Assemblies:

_____ 3. Measure the gearset endplay/clearance if required.
Tip: Excess gearset clearance indicates worn thrust washers.

Gearset clearance, Measured: _____,
Specification: _____
OK _____ **NOT OK** _____

_____ 4. Remove the retaining ring if necessary, and separate the gearset components.

All units:

_____ 5. Clean the components, and visually inspect them for wear.
Tip: Damaged or worn thrust washers should be replaced.

Sun Gear(s):	**OK** _____	**NOT OK** _____
Sun Gear Drive Shell:	**OK** _____	**NOT OK** _____
Ring Gear(s):	**OK** _____	**NOT OK** _____
Carrier(s):	**OK** _____	**NOT OK** _____
Planet Gears:	**OK** _____	**NOT OK** _____
Thrust Washers:	**OK** _____	**NOT OK** _____
Other _____	**OK** _____	**NOT OK** _____

← EXCESS CLEARANCE

_____ 6. Using a feeler gauge, measure the side clearance on every planet gear. Also, check each planet gear to make sure that it spins freely.
Tip: Use a feeler gauge size equal to the largest allowable clearance; if it enters there is too much clearance, probably from a worn thrust washer.

Side/thrust clearance, Measured: _____
Specification: _____
Free movement: OK _____ **NOT OK** _____

_____ 7. Some components have an internal bushing. Measure the bushing ID/shaft clearance.

Bushing clearance, Measured: _____ **Specification:** _____

Gearset Assemblies:

_____ 8. Lubricate all of the bearing and thrust surfaces using transmission assembly lube or petroleum jelly, and assemble the gearset. Install any retaining rings, and check to insure that it is properly seated.

OK _____ **NOT OK** _____

E 48, DISASSEMBLE, INSPECT, AND REASSEMBLE VALVE BODY

Meets NATEF Task: (C-3) Inspect, measure, clean, and replace valve body (includes surfaces, bores, springs, valves, sleeves, retainers, brackets, check-valves/balls, screens, spacers, and gaskets). (P-2)

Name_____ Date_____

Make/Model_____ Year_____ Instructor's OK _____

Note: The major components of an automatic transmission are normally serviced separately. They are disassembled, inspected, and reassembled using new or reconditioned parts as needed.

_____ 1. Identify the transmission.

Transmission make: _____ **Model:** _____

_____ 2. Locate the manufacturer's valve body repair procedure.
Tip: *Valve body service is described in textbook Chapter 18.*

Information source: _____ **Section:** _____ **Date:** _____
Print or photocopy the valve body illustration: Yes _____ No _____

Disassembly:

_____ 3. Remove the valve retainers (pins, clips, covers). Remove each valve, one at a time, along with its plug, sleeve, and spring. Note that the valve should slide freely out of its bore. Record any sticky or sloppy valves.

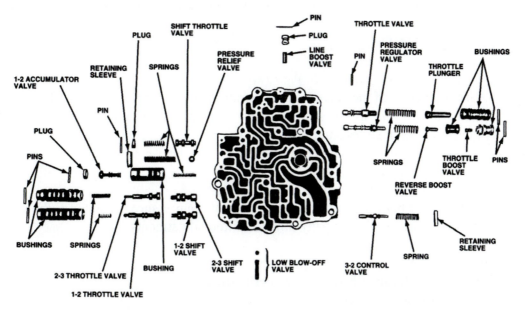

Tip: *It is recommended that you get a copy of an exploded view of the valve body.*

Identify each valve and the related parts as they are removed; pay special attention to the spring color, size, or number of coils. Remember that you need to become the expert on this particular valve body.

Tip: *If a valve body diagram is not available, carefully lay out the valves and springs to keep them in order or draw your own diagram as you disassemble the valve body.*

Tip: *A simple valve holder can be made by folding a sheet of heavy paper into a series of V-folds.*

OK _____ **NOT OK** _____, **Sticking valves:** _____

_____ 4. Thoroughly clean the valve body, valves, transfer plate, and any other parts.

Inspection:
_____ 5. Visually inspect the parts for wear or damage.

Valve Body: **OK** _____ **NOT OK** _____, **explain** _____
Valves: **OK** _____ **NOT OK** _____, **explain** _____
Valve Sleeves: **OK** _____ **NOT OK** _____, **explain** _____
Valve Plugs: **OK** _____ **NOT OK** _____, **explain** _____
Springs: **OK** _____ **NOT OK** _____, **explain** _____
Transfer Plate: **OK** _____ **NOT OK** _____, **explain** _____
Filter Screens: **OK** _____ **NOT OK** _____, **explain** _____
Check Balls: **OK** _____ **NOT OK** _____, **explain** _____

Tip: *If a valve has a small burr, the burr can be removed using a sharpening stone.* ***Never*** *use an abrasive material on an aluminum valve.*

_____ 6. Some valve bodies are prone to wear the bore, which causes fluid pressure loss. Wiggle the valve up and down; perceptible movement can indicate a worn bore.

Tip: *A bore reamer and oversize valve can be used to repair some valve bodies.*

OK _____ **NOT OK** _____

Assembly:
_____ 7. Use your copy of the valve body illustration, and assemble the valve body, Lubricate each valve with ATF as you slide them into the bore. Test each assembled valve by making sure that it slides smoothly in its bore.

OK _____ **NOT OK** _____

_____ 8. Some valve bodies require an adjustment of the pressure regulator as the valve body is assembled. Perform this and any other required adjustments.

Adjustable? Yes _____ **Not Applicable** _____
Pressure regulator adjustment: Specification: _____
Other adjustments? Yes_____ **No**_____

E 49, DISASSEMBLE, INSPECT, AND REASSEMBLE DIFFERENTIAL

Meets NATEF Task: (C-17) Inspect, measure, repair, adjust, or replace transaxle final drive components. (P-2)

Name_____ Date_____

Make/Model_____ Year_____ Instructor's OK _____

Note: The major components of an automatic transaxle are normally serviced separately. They are disassembled, inspected, and reassembled using new or reconditioned parts as needed.

_____ 1. Identify the transaxle.

Transaxle make: _____ **Model:** _____

_____ 2. Locate the manufacturer's differential repair procedure.
Tip: Differential service is described in textbook Chapter 18.

Information source: _____
Section: _____
Date: _____

Disassembly:

_____ 3. Remove the ring gear, if required, and measure the side gear clearance/ backlash.
Tip: Excessive clearance indicates severe wear of the case, thrust washers, or gears.

Side gear clearance:
Specification: _____,
Measured: _____
OK _____ NOT OK _____

_____ 4. Remove the differential pinion shaft lock pin, and slide the shaft out of the case. Remove the pinion gears, side gears, and thrust washers from the case.

_____ 5. Thoroughly clean all of the parts.

Ring Gear Differential Pinion Shaft
Case
Side Gear
Pinion Gear

Inspection:

_____ 6. Visually inspect the parts for wear or damage.

Case: **OK** _____ **NOT OK** _____
Pinion Shaft: **OK** _____ **NOT OK** _____
Pinion Gears: **OK** _____ **NOT OK** _____
Side Gears: **OK** _____ **NOT OK** _____
Thrust Washers: OK _____ **NOT OK** _____
Lock Pin: **OK** _____ **NOT OK** _____

Tip: If the side gear clearance (Step 3) was excessive and thrust washers are used, new thrust washers might reduce the amount to an acceptable clearance.
Tip: Severely damaged parts normally require replacement of the differential assembly.

Assembly:

_____ 7. Lubricate the bearing surfaces, and assemble the differential.

OK _____ **NOT OK** _____

_____ 8. Remeasure the side gear clearance/backlash (Step 3).
Tip: Excessive clearance can be reduced using a new washer or a thicker thrust washer, which is available for some differentials.

Side gear clearance: Specification: _____ Measured: _____
OK _____ **NOT OK** _____

_____ 9. Install the ring gear on the case, if it was removed. Install the bolts evenly, and tighten them to the specified torque.
Tip: Some ring gears fit tightly onto the case; installation is easier if the ring gear is heated to about 212°F (100°C).

Bolt torque specification: _____

E 50, DISASSEMBLE, INSPECT, AND REASSEMBLE SERVO AND BAND

Meets NATEF Task: (C-4 & 22) Inspect servo and bores, pistons, seals, pins, springs, and retainers; determine necessary action. (P-2)

Name_____ Date_____

Make/Model_____ Year_____ Instructor's OK _____

Note: The major components of an automatic transmission are normally serviced separately. They are disassembled, inspected, and reassembled using new or reconditioned parts as needed.

_____ 1. Identify the transmission.

Transmission make: _____
Model: _____

_____ 2. Locate the manufacturer's servo and band repair procedure.
Tip: *Seal and band service is described in textbook Chapter 17.*

Information source: _____
Section: _____ **Page:** _

Servo Disassembly:

_____ 3. Use the proper compressor to compress the servo return spring, remove the retainer ring, and carefully release the spring compressor. Remove the servo cover, piston, and spring.

_____ 4. Inspect the servo parts and the case servo bore for damage.
Tip: *A kit is available to repair a worn servo bore. It contains a sleeve to repair the servo bore, a piston, and piston seals.*

Servo Assembly:

_____ 5. Install new seals on the servo piston and a new seal or gasket on the servo cover.

_____ 6. Lubricate the piston and bore using automatic transmission assembly lube, petroleum jelly, or ATF. Slide the piston and spring into the bore. Place the cover in position, and using the proper compressor, compress the servo as required.

_____ 7. Install the servo cover retainer /bolts, and carefully release the spring compressor.

OK _____ NOT OK _____

Band Inspection:

_____ 8. If the band is to be reused, check it for these possible faults:

Lining condition:	OK _____	NOT OK _____
Lining wear:	OK _____	NOT OK _____
Lining contamination:	OK _____	NOT OK _____
Band end lugs:	OK _____	NOT OK _____

Drum Inspection:

_____ 9. Inspect the drum surface for these possible defects:
Tip: Stamped steel drums can be dished or be squeezed inward.
Tip: Worn or damaged drums should be resurfaced or replaced.

Scoring:	OK _____	NOT OK _____
Bluing/discoloring:	OK _____	NOT OK _____
Dishing:	OK _____	NOT OK _____

E 51, INSPECT AND REPAIR CASE

Meets NATEF Task: (C-15) Inspect case bores, passages, bushings, vents, and mating surfaces; determine necessary action. (P-2)

Name_____ Date_____

Make/Model_____ Year_____ Instructor's OK _____

Note: The major components of an automatic transmission are normally serviced separately. The individual components are disassembled, inspected, and reassembled using new or reconditioned parts as needed.

_____ 1. Identify the transmission.

Transmission make: _____ **Model:** _____

_____ 2. Locate the manufacturer's case inspection and repair procedure.
Tip: Case service is described in textbook Chapter 18.

Information source: _____ **Section:** _____ **Page:** _____

_____ 3. Thoroughly clean the case, and blow air through every oil passage to make sure they are clean. Blow air into every bolt thread cavity to remove all debris.
Tip: If the transmission has experienced a failure that could have been cause by a fluid pressure loss, close off the end of the suspect passage to test for an internal leak.

OK _____
NOT OK _____

Bolt Threads
Clutch Splines
Fluid Passages
Bushing

_____ 4. Inspect any clutch piston cavities for cracks or other damage.

OK _____ NOT OK _____ NA (not applicable) _____

_____ 5. Inspect the splined clutch plate lug areas for excessive lug wear.

OK _____ **NOT OK** _____ **NA** _____

_____ 6. Many cases include a rear bushing; inspect the bushing for wear or damage.
Tip: Damaged bushings should be replaced (see E 33).

OK _____ **NOT OK** _____ **NA** _____

_____ 7. Some cases include worm tracks for fluid passage in and out of the valve body; inspect this area for dents across the tracks, cracks, and warpage.
Tip: A warped case can be repaired by draw filing the area to make it flat.

OK _____ **NOT OK** _____ **NA** _____

_____ 8. Some cases include a governor bore; carefully inspect the bore for wear or damage.
OK _____ **NOT OK** _____ **NA** _____

_____ 9. Check all internal bolt threads for stripped or damaged threads.
Tip: Damaged bolt threads should be repaired by installing a thread insert (E 36).

OK _____ **NOT OK** _____

_____10. Remove and replace all external seals, such as the manual shift lever shaft seal.

OK _____ **NOT OK** _____

_____11. If the park is linkage still in the case, check the linkage, pawl, and spring for proper operation.

OK _____ **NOT OK** _____

E 52, INSPECT ONE-WAY CLUTCH, SHAFTS, AND INTERNAL SEALS

Meets NATEF Task: (C-21) Inspect roller and sprag clutches, races, rollers, sprags, springs, cages, and retainers; determine necessary action. (P-1)

Name_____ **Date**_____

Make/Model_____ **Year**_____ **Instructor's OK** _____

Note: The major components of an automatic transmission are normally serviced separately. They are disassembled, inspected, and reassembled using new or reconditioned parts as needed.

_____ 1. Identify the transmission.

Transmission make: _____ **Model:** _____

_____ 2. Locate the manufacturer's inspection procedure.

Information source: _____ **Section:** _____ **Date:** _____

One-Way Clutch:
_____ 3. **Roller Clutch:** Inspect the parts for wear or damage.

Cam:
OK _____ NOT OK _____ NA _____
Smooth Race:
OK _____ NOT OK _____ NA _____
Rollers:
OK _____ NOT OK _____ NA _____
Energizer Springs:
OK _____ NOT OK _____ NA _____

_____ 4. **Sprag Clutch:** Inspect the sprag for damage and improper sprag position and the races for wear or damage: *Tip: Most sprag clutches are an assembly that should not be taken apart.*

Sprag Assembly:
OK _____ NOT OK _____ NA _____
Inner Race:
OK _____ NOT OK _____ NA _____
Outer Race:
OK _____ NOT OK _____ NA _____

Input and Main/Output Shafts:

_____ 5. Inspect the bushing and seal ring areas for wear and damage; check all oil passages to make sure that they are clean.

Bushing races:	**OK** _____	**NOT OK** _____
Seal grooves:	**OK** _____	**NOT OK** _____
Oil passages:	**OK** _____	**NOT OK** _____

Internal Seals:

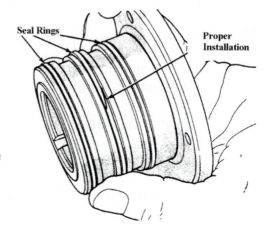

_____ 6. **Cut Sealing Rings:** Place the sealing rings into their grooves, making sure that the ends meet properly.
Continuous/Uncut Rings: Using the proper installing tool, slide the ring into position, and resize/squeeze the ring into the groove using the proper resizing tool.
Tip: Uncut Teflon rings are easier to install if they are warm.
Tip: Sealing ring service is described in textbook Chapter 17.

OK _____ **NOT OK** _____

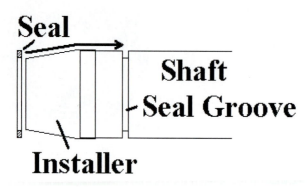

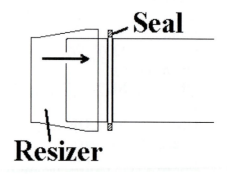

E 53, INSPECT TORQUE CONVERTER

Meets NATEF Task: (C-7) Inspect converter flex (drive) plate, converter attaching bolts, converter pilot converter pump drive surfaces, converter end play, and crankshaft pilot bore. (P-2)

Name_____ **Date**_____

Make/Model_____ **Year**_____ **Instructor's OK** _____

Note: The major components of an automatic transmission are normally serviced separately. They are disassembled, inspected, and reassembled using new or reconditioned parts as needed. Faulty torque converters can be rebuilt or replaced with a new or factory rebuilt unit.

_____ 1. Identify the transmission.

Transmission make: _____ **Model:** _____

_____ 2. Locate the manufacturer's torque converter inspection procedure.
Tip: Torque converter service is described in Chapter 19 of the textbook.

Information source: _____ **Section:** _____ **Page:** _____

_____ 3. Check the outside of the converter for indications of fluid leaks. Pay special attention to all of the welds.

OK _____ **NOT OK** _____

_____ 4. Clean the converter, and inspect/check for these possible defects.

Drive lugs/studs thread damage: OK _____ NOT OK _____
Pilot damage: OK _____ NOT OK _____
Hub wear or scoring: OK _____ NOT OK _____
Pump drive tang damage:
OK _____ NOT OK _____
Starter ring gear damage:
OK _____ NOT OK _____ NA _____

_____ 5. Check the stator clutch.
Tip: The stator reaction shaft splines should rotate freely in one direction and be locked in the other.

Lockup: OK _____ NOT OK _____
Freewheel: OK _____ NOT OK _____

_____ 6. Measure turbine end play.

Turbine End Play:
Specification: _____ **Measured:** _____

_____ 7. Check for internal interference.
Tip: Rotate the turbine and then the stator with the front of the converter in a downward position and then in an upward position.

Front end down: OK _____ **NOT OK** _____
Front end up: OK _____ **NOT OK** _____

_____ 8. Check for leaks.
Tip: Special fixtures are required to pressurize the converter to 30--40 psi (207 to 275 kPa) as you inspect for leaks.

OK _____ **NOT OK** _____

_____ 9. If the equipment is available, check the converter clutch.

OK _____ **NOT OK** _____
Unable to test _____

_____ 10. Check the flexplate for cracks and other damage.

OK _____ **NOT OK** _____

_____ 11. If the converter has been rebuilt or replaced, check the fit between the converter pilot and the crankshaft recess.
Tip: The pilot should have a snug fit into the recess bore.

OK _____ **NOT OK** _____

E 54, ASSEMBLE REAR WHEEL DRIVE (RWD) TRANSMISSION

Meets NATEF Task: (C-5) Assemble transmission/transaxle. (P-1)

Name_____ Date_____

Make/Model_____ Year_____ Instructor's OK _____

Note: As an automatic transmission is assembled, all of the components must be clean, all gaskets and seals should be replaced, and every rotating part should be lubricated.

_____ 1. Identify the transmission.

Transmission make: _____ **Model:** _____

_____ 2. Locate the manufacturer's transmission assembly procedure.
Tip: Transmission assembly is described in textbook Chapter 16.

Information source: _____, **Section:** _____, **Date:** _____

_____ 3. Install the gearset and clutch packs making sure that each component seats properly and rotates in the proper direction.

Tip: Every one-way clutch should be checked to insure that it locks and freewheels correctly.
Tip: Thrust washers can be held in position using transmission assembly lube or petroleum jelly.

_____ 4. Install the band(s) and servo(s), if used. Install case-mounted accumulators.
Tip: Many automatic transmissions require that bands be checked and adjusted. The band is usually adjusted by measuring the servo travel to determine the proper servo pin length.

_____ 5. Install the pump and gasket, tighten two of the mounting bolts to the correct torque, and measure gear train end play. Adjust the end play if necessary.

Tip: End play is normally adjusted by selecting the appropriate thrust washer.
Tip: Guide pins can be used to keep the pump gasket in position as the pump is installed.
Tip: If the gearset binds up as the pump bolts are tightened, check that the thrust washers are properly positioned and that the clutch is completely installed.

Measured end play: _____ **Specified end play:** _____

_____ 6. Air check each clutch and band servo to make sure that they apply and release properly. Identify each clutch and band and its condition in the chart below.
Tip: You should be able to hear the application of a clutch or band as air is applied.

Clutch 1: _____ **: OK** _____ **NOT OK** _____
Clutch 2: _____ **: OK** _____ **NOT OK** _____
Clutch 3: _____ **: OK** _____ **NOT OK** _____
Clutch 4: _____ **: OK** _____ **NOT OK** _____
Clutch 5: _____ **: OK** _____ **NOT OK** _____
Band 1: _____ **: OK** _____ **NOT OK** _____
Band 1: _____ **: OK** _____ **NOT OK** _____

_____ 7. Install the valve body using a new gasket(s) (E 38).

_____ 8. Install the shift and park linkage. Make sure that the parking pawl engages and disengages the tooth notches.

OK _____ **NOT OK** _____

_____ 9. Install the pan(s) and extension housing. Install the bolts, and tighten them to the specified torque.

_____ 10. Install any remaining exterior components.

E 55, ASSEMBLE FRONT WHEEL DRIVE (FWD) TRANSAXLE

Meets NATEF Task: (C-5) Assemble transmission/transaxle. (P-1)

Name_____ **Date**_____

Make/Model_____ **Year**_____ **Instructor's OK**_____

Note: As a transaxle is assembled, the components must be clean, all gaskets and seals should be replaced, and every rotating part should be lubricated.

_____ 1. Identify the transaxle.

Transmission make: _____ **Model:** _____

_____ 2. Locate the manufacturer's transaxle assembly procedure.
Tip: Transaxle assembly is described in textbook Chapter 16.

Information source: _____ **Section:** _____ **Page:** _____

_____ 3. Install the differential, gearset, and clutch packs. Check that each component seats properly and will rotate in the proper direction.
Tip: Every one-way clutch should be checked to insure that it locks and freewheels correctly.
Tip: Thrust washers can be held in position using automatic transmission assembly lube or petroleum jelly.

_____ 4. If required, adjust the bearing preload; all components that use tapered roller bearings require a bearing adjustment.
Tip: Bearing preload is usually adjusted using a selective shim at the bearing, cup, or retainer.

OK_____ **NOT OK**_____

_____ 5. Install the band(s) and servo(s), if used. Install any case-mounted accumulators.
Tip: Many modern automatic transmissions require that the band be adjusted during assembly. This is done by measuring the servo travel and selecting a servo pin of the proper length.

_____ 6. Install the pump and gasket. Tighten two of the mounting bolts to the correct torque. Measure the gear train end play, and adjust the end play if necessary.

Tip: End play is normally adjusted by replacing the appropriate selective thrust washer.

Tip: Guide pins can be used to keep the pump gasket in position as the pump is installed.

Tip: If the gearset binds up as the pump bolts are tightened, check for a misplaced thrust washer or a clutch that is not installed completely.

Measured end play: _____

Specified end play: _____

_____ 7. Air check each clutch and band servo to make sure that they apply and release properly. Identify each clutch and band and indicate their condition.

Tip: You can hear the clutch or band move as air is applied to it.

Clutch 1: _____ : **OK** _____ **NOT OK** _____
Clutch 2: _____ : **OK** _____ **NOT OK** _____
Clutch 3: _____ : **OK** _____ **NOT OK** _____
Clutch 4: _____ : **OK** _____ **NOT OK** _____
Clutch 5: _____ : **OK** _____ **NOT OK** _____
Band 1: _____ : **OK** _____ **NOT OK** _____
Band 1: _____ : **OK** _____ **NOT OK** _____

_____ 8. Install the valve body using a new gasket(s) (E 38).

_____ 9. Install the shift and park linkage. Make sure that the parking pawl engages and disengages the park gear notches.

OK _____ **NOT OK** _____

_____ 9. Install the pan(s) and extension housing. Install the bolts, and tighten them to the specified torque.

_____ 10. Install any remaining exterior components.

Appendix 1

DRIVE TRAIN SAFETY PRECAUTIONS

- Always wear protective eye wear and clothing (including hand protection) when working on vehicles.
- Stay clear of moving engine and vehicle parts such as drive belts and driveshafts.
- Refer to the appropriate material safety data sheet (MSDS) when working with each new chemical so you become familiar with the properties of that chemical.
- Always set the parking brake, and place secure blocks at the front and back of the tires before working on a vehicle.
- Always follow the directions of the lift, jack, and /or vehicle manufacturer when lifting a vehicle for undercar service.
- Always make sure that the vehicle is securely supported before performing undercar service.
- Never overfill an automatic transmission with fluid: the fluid can spill onto a hot exhaust and cause a fire.
- If checking fluid pressure using a gauge with a rubber hose, make sure the hose is in good condition and routed away from hot or moving parts.
- Avoid contact with hot parts of a vehicle such as the catalytic converter, exhaust pipe, and radiator.
- Always clean up any fluid spills as soon as possible.
- When cleaning parts, direct high pressure air away from yourself and others.
- Do not smoke while working on a vehicle.
- Remove metal jewelry and loose clothing before working on a vehicle.
- Disconnect the battery ground cable first, before making undercar repairs that might cause starter engagement or contact with electrical terminals. Make sure that the ignition is turned off before disconnecting the battery.
- Be aware that vehicle electrical systems can cause a shock, especially on 42 volt and higher systems. The higher voltages can cause a fatal shock.
- Remember that if a wrench, screwdriver, metal tool, or jewelry creates an electrical short circuit, the resulting spark can cause a fire, produce burns, and severely damage the metal parts involved.
- If working under an instrument panel, be aware that probing the wrong wire can cause airbag deployment, even with a disconnected battery. Besides being very expensive, airbag deployment can cause serious injury. Never probe a yellow or orange wire unless directed to.

Appendix 2, NATEF Task Check List, 2008

NATEF Automatic Transmission and Transaxle Task	Exercise	Date Completed	Instructor's OK
A. General Transmission and Transaxle Diagnosis			
1. Complete work order to include customer information, vehicle identifying information, customer concern, related service history, cause, and correction. (P-1)	E 3		
2. Identify and interpret transmission/transaxle concern; differentiate between engine performance and transmission/transaxle concerns; determine necessary action. (P-1)	E 16 to 26		
3. Research applicable vehicle and service information, such as transmission/transaxle system operation, fluid type, vehicle service history, service precautions, and technical service bulletins. (P-1)	E 4 & 5		
4. Locate and interpret vehicle and major component identification numbers. (P-1)	E 4		
5. Diagnose fluid loss and condition concerns; check fluid level in transmissions with and without dip-stick; determine necessary action. (P-1)	E 6, 7 & 9		
6. Perform pressure tests (including transmissions/transaxles equipped with electronic pressure control); determine necessary action. (P-1)	E 19 & 22		
7. Perform stall test; determine necessary action. (P-1)	E 20		
8. Perform lock-up converter tests; determine necessary action. (P-1)	E 23		
9. Diagnose noise and vibration concerns; determine necessary action. (P-2)	E 18		
10. Diagnose transmission/transaxle gear reduction/ multiplication concerns using driving, driven, and held member (power flow) principles. (P-1)	E 18		
11. Diagnose pressure concerns in the transmission using hydraulic principles (Pascal's Law). (P-2)	E 19		
12. Diagnose electronic transmission/transaxle control systems using appropriate test equipment and service information. (P-2)	E 13, 14 & 15		
B. In-Vehicle Transmission/Transaxle Maintenance and Repair			
1. Inspect, adjust, or replace manual valve shift linkage, transmission range sensor/switch, and park/neutral position switch. (P-2)	E 10 & 11		

NATEF Task	Exercise	Date Completed	Instructor's OK
2. Inspect and replace external seals, gaskets, and bushings. (P-2)	E 34		
3. Inspect, test, adjust, repair, or replace electrical/electronic components, and circuits, including computers, solenoids, sensors, relays, terminals, connectors, switches, and harnesses. (P-1)	E 25, 26 & 27		
4. Diagnose electronic transmission control systems using a scan tool; determine necessary action. (P-1)	E 25 & 26		
5. Inspect, replace, and align powertrain mounts. (P-2)	E 35		
6. Service transmission; perform visual inspection; replace fluid and filters. (P-1)	E 6, 7, 8 & 9		
C. Off-Vehicle Transmission and Transaxle Repair			
1. Remove and reinstall transmission/transaxle and torque converter; inspect engine core plugs, rear crankshaft seal, dowel pins, dowel pin holes, and mating surfaces. (P-1)	E 39, 40, 41 & 42		
2. Disassemble, clean, and inspect transmission/transaxle. (P-1)	E 43 & 44		
3. Inspect, measure, clean, and replace valve body (includes surfaces, bores, springs, valves, sleeves, retainers, brackets, check-valves/balls, screens, spacers, and gaskets). (P-2)	E 38 & 48		
4. Inspect servo and accumulator bores, pistons, seals, pins, springs, and retainers; determine necessary action. (P-2)	E 50 & 51		
5. Assemble transmission/transaxle. (P-1)	E 54 & 55		
6. Inspect, leak test, and flush or replace transmission/ transaxle oil cooler, lines, and fittings. (P-1)	E 24 & 37		
7. Inspect converter flex (drive) plate, converter attaching bolts, converter pilot, converter pump drive surfaces, converter end play, and crankshaft pilot bore. (P-2)	E 45 & 53		
8. Install and seat torque converter to engage drive splines. (P-1)	E 41 & 42		
9. Inspect, measure, and reseal oil pump assembly and components. (P-1)	E 45		
10. Measure transmission/transaxle end play or preload; determine necessary action. (P-1)	E 43, 44, 54, & 55		
11. Inspect, measure, and replace thrust washers and bearings. (P-2)	E 47, 54 & 55		
12. Inspect oil delivery circuits, including seal rings, ring grooves, and sealing surface areas, feed pipes, orifices, and check valves/balls. (P-2)	E 52		

NATEF Task	Exercise	Date Completed	Instructor's OK
13. Inspect bushings; determine necessary action. (P-2)	E 33		
14. Inspect and measure planetary gear assembly components; determine necessary action. (P-2)	E 47		
15. Inspect case bores, passages, bushings, vents, and mating surfaces; determine necessary action. (P-2)	E 51		
16. Inspect transaxle drive, link chains, sprockets, gears, bearings, and bushings; perform necessary action. (P-2)	E 44		
17. Inspect, measure, repair, adjust, or replace transaxle final drive components. (P-2)	E 49		
18. Inspect clutch drum, piston, check-balls, springs, retainers, seals, and friction and pressure plates; determine necessary action. (P-2)	E 46		
19. Measure clutch pack clearance; determine necessary action. (P-1)	E 46		
20. Air test operation of clutch and servo assemblies. (P-1)	E 22 & 46		
21. Inspect roller and sprag clutch, races, rollers, sprags, springs, cages, and retainers; determine necessary action. (P-1)	E 52		
22. Inspect bands and drums; determine necessary action. (P-2)	E 50		
23. Describe the operational characteristics of a continuously variable transmission (CVT). (P-3)	WS 8		
24. Describe the operational characteristics of a hybrid vehicle drive train. (P-3)	WS 9		

Note: WS = Work Sheet which is part of the Instructor's Manual

WHY DO REPLACEMENT SEALS FAIL EARLY?

Several problems can cause early failure of an oil seal that has been replaced. Remember that worn bearings will allow the shaft to move sideways, and this can produce seal leaks.

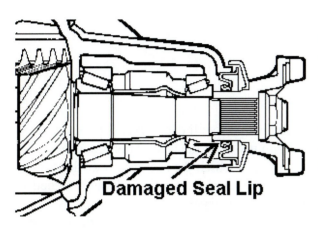

Damaged Seal Lip

The seal lip can be cut or damaged during installation as the item it seals against (in this case, the U-joint flange/yoke) is being installed. Another cause can be a worn, rough, scratched surface on the yoke, which is the inner sealing surface. Many technicians thoroughly clean the yoke surface using a fine abrasive pad. Both the sealing lip and the yoke sealing surface should be lubricated before the flange is installed.

If the retaining nut is not tightened to the correct torque, the flange can move back and forth on the pinion shaft. This will produce a pumping action at the seal and move fluid under it. Tighten the pinion nut too tight and the bearings will be overloaded and the crush sleeve spacer will become too short. Worn bearings can also cause this leak.

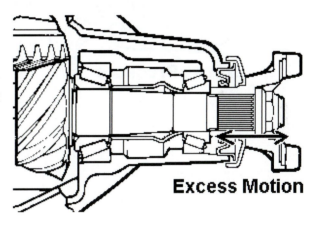

Excess Motion

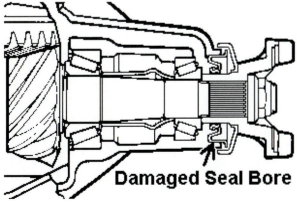

Damaged Seal Bore

A groove or deep scratch can be cut in the seal bore so fluid can leak past the seal's outer edge. This is often the result of sloppy seal removal. If you find this damage, coat the seal housing with a film of RTV sealant. Sloppy seal installation can also dent or scratch the seal housing and cause this type of leak.

Fluid can leak down the splines between the pinion shaft and the flange. Technicians can prevent this by cleaning the splines and the back of the washer retaining the flange. A thin film of sealant on the pinion shaft splines and the back side of the washer will help prevent this leak.

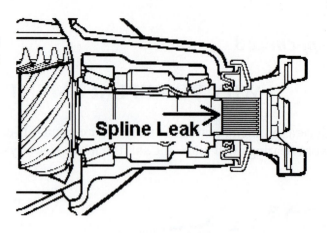

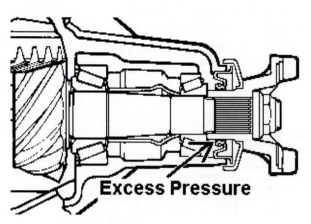

A plugged vent will cause excess pressure to build up inside of the case. This produces a condition in which the seal has to work against a pressure that is greater than it was designed to hold. You can check for this condition by seeing if there is pressure inside of the case as you remove the fluid level plug; there should be none. Another check is to remove the vent and try blowing through it; you should be able to blow through the vent.